NEW DIRECTIONS FOR MENTAL HEALTH SERVICES

H. Richard Lamb, *University of Southern California*
EDITOR-IN-CHIEF

The Role of the State Hospital in the Twenty-First Century

William D. Spaulding
University of Nebraska-Lincoln

EDITOR

Number 84, Winter 1999

JOSSEY-BASS PUBLISHERS
San Francisco

The Role of the State Hospital in the Twenty-First Century
William D. Spaulding (ed.)
New Directions for Mental Health Services, no. 84
H. Richard Lamb, Editor-in-Chief

Microfilm copies of issues and articles are available in 16mm and 35mm, as well as microfiche in 105mm, through University Microfilms Inc., 300 North Zeeb Road, Ann Arbor, Michigan 48106-1346.

ISSN 0193-9416 ISBN 0-7879-1433-9

New Directions for Mental Health Services is part of The Jossey-Bass Psychology Series and is published quarterly by Jossey-Bass Inc., Publishers, 350 Sansome Street, San Francisco, California 94104-1342.

Subscriptions cost $65.00 for individuals and $110.00 for institutions, agencies, and libraries.

Editorial correspondence should be sent to the Editor-in-Chief, H. Richard Lamb, University of Southern California, Department of Psychiatry, Graduate Hall, 1937 Hospital Place, Los Angeles, California 90033-1071.

Cover photograph by Wernher Krutein/PHOTOVAULT © 1990.

Jossey-Bass Web address: www.josseybass.com

Printed in the United States of America on acid-free recycled paper containing 100 percent recovered waste paper, of which at least 20 percent is postconsumer waste.

CONTENTS

Editor's Notes

Do we still need state hospitals? Can they be completely replaced by community-based services? A bemused director of a community mental health center pondered these questions:

> There's the county nursing home. It has over 300 beds. When people go there, they seldom leave before they die. It is a self-contained operation, having virtually everything its residents may need within its walls. But it's a *community-based facility*. Less than a mile down the street is the state hospital. It has about 150 beds, about a third of which are for brief periods of hospitalization. Most of the rest of the beds are in rehabilitative programs geared to return patients to less restrictive programs or even their own homes in the shortest possible period of time. There is extensive coordination of services between those programs, the community mental health center, and private providers. It even has a transitional program, jointly staffed by the state hospital, the community mental health center, and a private provider. But it's not a *community-based facility*—it's an *institution*.[1]

How can any debate be resolved when language and terminology mean so little? There is no question that developments in biomedical and psychosocial technologies over the past several decades have had an enormous impact on the need for long-term care in public psychiatric institutions. However, this has led to more, not less, debate about what specific services are really needed and how exactly state hospitals can potentially serve this need. Part of the problem is that "state hospital" has come to have connotations not shared by all parties to the debate. Is a state hospital always a specific physical facility? Is it by definition *not* a community-based resource? Does it duplicate services that could be provided better in the private sector? Is it by definition a more restrictive environment than *any* community-based program? Does it necessarily and inevitably drain funding away from community-based services? A state hospital of the future could conceivably have none of these characteristics and in fact could employ clinical technology that isn't in use in today's state hospitals and that couldn't be used in other settings. But this recalls the parable of the old woodsman who observed that he'd used the same ax for fifty years, though he'd replaced the head twice and the handle five times.

Complicating these semantic entanglements is debate that blurs the boundary between science and ideology. This is perhaps inevitable, inasmuch as severe and disabling mental illness is a social and cultural phenomenon as well as a biomedical and behavioral one. The infusion of ideology has produced a somewhat polarized configuration of beliefs and perspectives, despite the polythetic convolutions and vicissitudes of more scientific and technological considerations. At one pole, there is the view that clinical technology now provides a complete alternative to state hospitals, that we no longer need them, that they cause more problems than they solve. At the other pole is the view that abandonment of state hospitals is abandonment of at least some people within the larger population of those with severe and disabling psychiatric disorders. Parties at both poles and at all points between express paramount concern for the safety, comfort, and humanity of the subject population. However, at times they may be concerned about different subject populations. Emotions sometimes run high. Expectations that this polarization would dissipate, in response to widespread acknowledgment in the late 1970s of the failures of the "first wave" of deinstitutionalization, which began in the 1960s, may have been too optimistic.

This issue of *New Directions for Mental Health Services* is a collection of chapters that address various aspects of the debate about the future of state hospitals. The editor makes no claim to have purged the content of ideological perspectives. Indeed, health care policy must ultimately be a synthesis of scientific, philosophical, technological, economic, political, and therefore ideological considerations. However, none of the chapters in this collection can be assigned to one or another of the aforementioned poles. On the one hand, they all convey a modicum of caution, even skepticism, about the notion that there is no longer a need for state hospital–based services, now or in the foreseeable future. On the other hand, there is no sympathy for the idea that state hospitals do not need to change. In the end, moderate ideological positions usually return the debate to increasingly specific, less impassioned, and more technological considerations, and that is the hoped-for outcome of this project.

This collection is divided into two parts. The first consists of chapters that express the perspectives of observers and participants at various levels of the mental health system, in a "top-down" progression. The initial contribution is by Leona L. Bachrach, internationally known as one of the most experienced, persistent, and insightful commentators on services for people with severe and disabling psychiatric disorders. Her analyses have been influential since the first wave of deinstitutionalization. Her perspective is a sociopsychological one that speaks to the society- and culturewide understandings and preconceptions that shape policy in this corner of the mental health arena. The next chapter, by Richard H. Hunter, conveys the perspective of a state government–level mental health administrator and provides useful, if troubling, insights about how politics and bureaucratic forces interact with clinical realities to shape the roles of state hospitals. The next two contributions are "case studies," not of individual patients but of state hospital–based rehabilitation programs. The first of these, by Paul Stuve and Anthony A. Menditto, recounts the history of a state hospital distinctive for its progressive treatment and rehabilitation, as the community-based system struggled to evolve around it. Similarly, the final chapter in the first part of the collection, by Mary Sullivan, describes the sixteen-year history of a progressive rehabilitation program *within* a more traditional state hospital. Her account describes the deconstruction and reconstruction of policy, as the program, its hospital, and its surrounding service system were thrown into the crucible of reform.

The second part of this collection includes contributions that more directly address the technological aspects of the future of state hospitals. The first of these, by Mario J. Scalora, is an analysis of the increasing role of forensic and related psycholegal factors, in mental health systems in general, and in state hospitals in particular. The next, by Eric B. Elbogen and Alan J. Tomkins, describes a new and rapidly evolving perspective on forensic and psycholegal issues called *therapeutic jurisprudence,* which could enhance, if not revolutionize, management of the most intractable problems in mental health services. The next contribution, by Maria B. Monroe-DeVita and Dennis F. Mohatt, is an analysis of community-based technologies that are already exerting a definitive impact on the role of state hospitals, Assertive Community Treatment, and related types of intensive case management. Their analysis shows that this defining impact must be expected to continue, not only because of the effectiveness of the approach for most of the severely and persistently mentally ill (SPMI) population but also because of its limitations. The final chapter in this section, by Brett Buican and colleagues, describes the state of the art in clinical data and information management technology, which not only will maximize the outcome of integrated hospital-community programs of the future but also may enable the very survival of such programs in managed care environments.

The final chapter in this volume is a formulation by the editor of the various issues addressed collectively by the preceding contributions. The formulation is a proposed prototype for an integration of the key technological and economic considerations and social values expected to determine the future of state hospitals.

Note

1. The editor is indebted to George Hanigan for this helpful insight.

William D. Spaulding
Editor

WILLIAM D. SPAULDING is professor of psychology in the Clinical Psychology Training Program at the University of Nebraska-Lincoln and clinical psychologist in the Community Transition Program, Lincoln Regional Center.

PART ONE

The Role of Policy

There is a core of services whose specific content varies from place to place that still appears to belong to the state mental hospital.

The State of the State Mental Hospital at the Turn of the Century

Leona L. Bachrach

In 1978, Maxwell Jones wrote, "I'm very worried about state hospitals, which I visit in many parts of the country. They are all demoralized and feel forgotten. The interest (and money) has moved to the new community programs which are not supplying the answer to chronic mental patients" (p. 610).

Over the past quarter-century, I have written at considerable length about the state of the state mental hospital in the United States. In a 1976 monograph entitled *Deinstitutionalization: An Analytical Review and Sociological Perspective* (Bachrach, 1976), I described the variety of functions, many of them subtle and unanticipated, that state mental hospitals had in the past performed and were continuing to execute even as community-based services were being rapidly developed. Some of those functions pertained to direct patient care; others had more to do with patients' families, service systems' priorities, and the demands of society at large. I suggested in that year that those functions were critical and could not productively be set aside, and I argued that successful *deinstitutionalization* would be dependent on communities' ability and willingness to assume the complete array of state mental hospital functions.

Ten years later in 1986, in an article in *Hospital and Community Psychiatry,* I wrote that although some communities had been more successful than others, the necessary transfer of state mental hospital functions to community agencies had been, at best, only partial (Bachrach, 1986b). I made four predictions—that the state hospital was destined to survive as an important service site for long-term mental patients into the foreseeable future; that, far from being monolithic,

This chapter is an update of an earlier publication: Bachrach, L. "The State of the State Mental Hospital in 1996." *Psychiatric Services,* 1996, 47 (12), 1071–1078.

its character would vary greatly among states and communities; that it would continue to serve as one of a variety of important loci of care for long-term mental patients; and that it was destined to be burdened by identity crises and financial shortfalls in the years to come. I also urged that so long as the state mental hospital was serving as a vital force in service delivery, it should be viewed as an integral part of the continuum of services for those patients.

Today, as a new millennium dawns, I continue to hold these views—views that are bolstered by documentation in a corpus of literature that continues to grow in spite of what some experts perceive as a diminishing role for the state mental hospital: nothing I have witnessed or read over the past quarter-century leads me to alter these positions in any material way. Yet as I prepare this chapter, I find myself more reluctant than I formerly was to suggest what the future might hold for state mental hospitals. The profound changes in service delivery that have accompanied the growth of managed care in recent years have been occurring so rapidly that it is too early to say how mentally ill persons will ultimately fare (Bachrach, 1986b). That we are in the midst of a health care revolution in the United States is obvious, and I, for one, am loath to attempt to anticipate its consequences for individuals who suffer from severe and persisting mental illnesses.

The purposes of this chapter are twofold—to update my previous writings on the topic of state mental hospitals and to provide some perspective that may be of assistance to the next generation of service planners, who surely have their work cut out for them. Citations from the current literature—including periodical articles suggested in Medline searches, newspaper reports, recent books on mental health service systems, and a variety of writings found in the "fugitive" literature, which is generally unindexed in traditional archives—will be interspersed with commentary and observations born of long professional interest in, and personal concern for, the fate of persons who suffer from long-term mental illnesses.

Four general and interrelated questions that recur in today's literature serve as the basis for this analytical review. These revolve around prevailing contemporary perceptions of state mental hospitals, the characteristics of the patients whom those facilities serve, the fate of those whom they no longer serve, and the appropriate role of state hospitals in today's systems of care. Although these questions represent but a portion of those discussed in the literature, I have selected them for their currency and for the frequency with which they are voiced, either explicitly or implicitly. Their popularity reveals that the controversy over state hospital care has not died and that despite continued downsizing and depopulation of these facilities over more than forty years, experts are still pondering their value for patients, their relevance to the greater system of care, and their overall viability.

Four Interrelated Questions

In this section, each of the four questions is examined.

Question One. *What is the prevailing view of state mental hospitals today, and how does it compare with the view that existed in the first half of this century?*

This critical question may be paraphrased in more direct, perhaps less polite, terms: Are today's state mental hospitals "any better" than those that existed in the first half of this century? Are they more or less humane, and are the services they offer more or less appropriate? These are difficult questions to answer, for state mental hospitals in the past were very diverse facilities that varied greatly in their milieus, their treatment offerings, and the competence of their personnel; and they continue to be so to this day. Were the semanticist S. I. Hayakawa (1972) to have written about these facilities, he might well have said then, as now, that "state $hospital_1$ is not state $hospital_2$."

Some state mental hospitals today, as in the past, house innovative programs for the care and rehabilitation of long-term mental patients (Ozarin, 1989; Smith, 1998). Others serve as gateway facilities in integrated systems of care (Shapiro, 1983). Others, however, though generally attending to patients' basic survival needs, appear to offer them little that fosters effective treatment, personal hope, or growth.

What is more, there are no standardized, universally accepted criteria by which to assess the character or quality of a given state mental hospital, let alone to compare entire categories of these facilities over different time periods.

It is, however, possible to say that state mental hospitals in various parts of the United States are today under severe attack for reported nontherapeutic and inhumane practices, even as they were in the 1950s. For example, according to the *New York Times* ("New Managers . . .," 1996, p. B5), a New Jersey state hospital recently experienced a "series of humiliating incidents," including patient suicides, staff negligence, and sexual assault of patients by staff members. In New York City in 1995, a violent, homicidal patient released from a state hospital pushed a woman to her death under a subway train—an incident that was widely viewed as the product of incompetent decision making within the hospital and that resulted in the dismissal of the state's acting commissioner of mental health (Dugger, 1995).

In the District of Columbia, patients at St. Elizabeths Hospital were forced for a period during the winter of 1995 to sleep in their coats because of a boiler malfunction (Harris, 1995). More recently, after a patient tumbled down a laundry chute to her death, St. Elizabeths was severely criticized for paying inadequate attention to the simple safety needs of its residents (Goldstein, 1997). A *Washington Post* article described that hospital as a place with "freezing wards, sporadic hot water, medication shortages, and inadequate staffing" (Strauss, 1996, p. A1, p. A5).

Similarly, the *Denver Post* asserted that the state mental hospital in Pueblo, in failing to provide individualized care for patients, had "triggered increases in the numbers of suicides, attempted suicides, assaults, sexual assaults and disciplinary measures involving seclusion or restraint" (Emery, Mitchell, and Lowe, 1998).

For many who recall the rhetoric of the early years of deinstitutionalization, there is a déjà vu quality both to these events and to the newspaper reports describing them: exposés of treatment deficits and inhumane living conditions inside state mental hospitals were common fare in those days. However, state mental hospitals even then had their supporters as well as their critics, and polarized views concerning the merits of deinstitutionalization were not uncommon.

By the early 1970s, it appeared that these views might be moderating (Bachrach, 1976). Dingman (1974) observed that many community-based facilities were being no more successful in meeting the needs of severely mentally ill individuals than were state hospitals, and he wrote that whatever the inherent problems of state hospital care might be, it was unthinkable to do away with them completely.

During the decade of the 1970s, concrete efforts to link state mental hospitals with community-based services in fact achieved some popularity in the United States in initiatives described as unified systems of care (Smith, Jones, and Coye, 1977; Stratas, Bernhardt, and Elwell, 1977; Talbott, 1983b). Perhaps, in retrospect, it was relatively easy in that decade to attempt to build systems of care that permitted the coexistence—even the active cooperation—of state mental hospitals and community-based agencies: it was a time when there seemed to be no limit to resources available for mental health services, and experimental initiatives were encouraged (Dinitz and Beran, 1971). But today's fierce competition for funding among mental health service entities (Freudenheim, 1995; Petrila, 1995) has led to something of a standoff, and it appears from the tenor of the most current literature that we are headed for a return to the either-or thinking of the early years of deinstitutionalization (Geller, 1997). I believe that part of the responsibility for this unfortunate situation lies in the indiscriminate condemnation of state hospital care by many decision makers—an ideological holdover from an earlier era (Jones, 1978).

There is thus no single predominant view of state mental hospitals today. Polarized reactions to the services rendered in these facilities—and even to their very presence as operating service sites for the care of long-term mental patients—prevail; and any progress, real or apparent, that might once have been made in bringing opposing views closer together is, at best, in abeyance.

Nor can we make valid comparisons between the state mental hospitals of today and yesteryear. Because we lack standardized criteria that would enable us to undertake such comparisons in any global manner, we are destined to abide by the limits imposed by historical canon; and we must assess these facilities only within, not across, time periods.

Question Two. *What individuals tend to be served in state mental hospitals today?*

Numerically speaking, the position of the state mental hospital in the spectrum of services for long-term mental patients has declined significantly over the past four decades (National Association of State Mental Health Program Directors, 1997; Witkin, Atay, and Manderscheid, 1996). Over a period of about forty years, there was a drop of approximately 86 percent in the number of resident patients in those facilities—from 560,000 people in 1955 to 77,000 people in the early years of this decade. Even more impressive is the decrease in resident patient rates: in 1955, 339 out of every 100,000 people living in the United States resided in state mental hospitals; early in this decade, only 31 of every 100,000 people were on those hospitals' rolls on any given day—a drop of well over 90 percent (Bachrach, 1986a; Center for Mental Health Services, 1995a).

Additional documentation for the declining presence of the state mental hospital in numerical terms is provided by comparative statistics on the location of patient care episodes. In 1955, 63 percent of all such episodes in the United States were conducted in state mental hospitals, in contrast to only 16 percent in 1990 (Redick, Witkin, Atay, and Manderscheid, 1994).

To some critics of the passing scene, the fact that more than 75,000 individuals continue to reside in state mental hospitals on any given day is probably regarded as excessive and as evidence that deinstitutionalization—the replacement of state mental hospitals with an array of community-based facilities for the care of severely mentally ill individuals (Bachrach, 1976)—has progressed neither far enough nor rapidly enough. To others, however, this figure establishes something of a threshold for the absolute limits of deinstitutionalization: it suggests that there is an irreducible minimum beyond which state mental hospital populations will not drop (Lamb, 1997; Thompson and others, 1993; Wines, 1988). To still others who view with alarm the growing populations of poorly served or totally unserved mentally ill individuals in our correctional facilities and on our streets (Butterfield, 1998; Center for Mental Health Services, 1995b; Friedrich and Flory, 1996; Isaac and Jaffe, 1996; Lamb and Weinberger, 1998; Lurigio and Lewis, 1989; Munetz and Geller, 1993; Satel, 1996; Teplin, 1990; Torrey, 1995), the number is perhaps far too small and might productively be increased to accommodate the needs of individuals who are largely overlooked in today's community-based systems of care.

Who is represented among the individuals who continue to use our state mental hospitals today? The actual number of users over the course of a year is substantially larger than the resident count on any one day; and generally speaking, the rolls of those facilities include, as they did in the past, measurable numbers of people in three major subgroups (Bachrach, 1978; Craig, Goodman, Siegel, and Wanderling, 1984; Wing, 1975):

Old long-stay patients individuals who have resided in the hospital for an extended period of time, generally more than one year but often in excess of five or ten years, and who are considered to be "poor risks" for discharge

New long-stay patients—recent first admissions who are unlikely to be released to the community

Short-stay patients—recently admitted patients who are likely to remain in residence for periods of only one or two weeks or even less and who often return to be readmitted in a "revolving-door" manner

Short-stay patients, particularly those with multiple admissions, represent a clear majority in many if not most facilities (Appleby and others, 1993; Fisher and others, 1996; Geller, 1992). However, the precise composition of state hospital populations varies greatly from facility to facility, and there are probably as many answers to the question of who is on the rolls of the state mental hospital as there are state hospitals. The sources of variance are complex, but several intertwined prominent conditions stand out.

First, the characteristics of mentally ill persons living in the geographic area served by a particular hospital must be taken into account. What is the distribution of these individuals according to diagnosis, symptomatology, level of functioning, demographic characteristics, ability to tolerate stress, and individual treatment history? Is the locale attracting transient severely mentally ill persons? Does it contain many homeless mentally ill people? Because all of these circumstances play a critical role in service utilization patterns, their distribution within the base population will to some extent determine who is admitted to, and who stays inside, a given state mental hospital.

Second, laws and regulations governing both inpatient and outpatient civil commitment of mentally ill persons vary among states, and these too have an influence on the composition of a state mental hospital's resident population (Isaac and Jaffe, 1996; Geller, 1986). In some catchment areas, the legal criteria for hospital admission, often restricted to dangerousness to one's self or others, are extremely rigid; and the "front doors" to those facilities are practically impossible to penetrate—a situation that has caused some service providers as well as family advocacy groups to react with dismay (Carr, 1992; Foderaro, 1994; Jaffe, 1995). Some state mental hospitals limit their admissions to involuntary commitments, but others—those located in communities that are relatively relaxed about admission criteria—contain greater percentages of people who have been voluntarily admitted. Some hospitals are actually reported to open their doors, albeit temporarily, to transient mentally ill persons who have traveled considerable distances from their homes (Bachrach 1988b).

A third set of variables affecting who uses the state hospital today is related to the array of alternative services actually available to severely mentally ill persons within the community. Individual places differ greatly in their service offerings as well as their gatekeeping practices; and to the extent that community agencies function as "trade-offs" for state hospitals, they too will influence the nature of the hospital's population. Some experts are persuaded that the emergence of managed care entities is today gravely limiting long-term patients' access to traditional services, both within the community and in state hospitals (Pinheiro, 1998).

Finally, a fourth set of circumstances that is critical in determining state hospital utilization patterns has to do with the community's goals in serving mentally ill individuals. Some communities are apparently less willing than others to tolerate the presence of these individuals (Lamb, Bachrach, and Kass, 1992). Some, for example, may be particularly sensitive to the existence of unserved, often homeless, mentally ill persons in their midst, and those that wish to minimize the presence of this population often turn to the state mental hospital as an alternative to providing no care at all. In some cases, the community's motives for using the state hospital in this manner may simply be intolerance and discrimination; in other instances, however, the hospital may genuinely be seen as a humane option for relieving the discomfort and pain experienced by many severely mentally ill persons in the community.

In a similar vein, the state mental hospital in some places has become the predominant treatment site for individuals who are violent, who appear to be dangerous to themselves or others, who have a history of incarceration, who are perceived as unable to care for themselves, or who are in some sense regarded as public nuisances. Numerous reports in the literature provide important clues to the characteristics of such "difficult-to-serve" individuals, who, not infrequently, end up on the state hospital's rolls in the absence of other facilities that will treat them (Bigelow and others, 1988; Casper, 1995; Fisher and others, 1996; Geller, 1992; Holohean, Banks, and Maddy, 1993; Lyons and others, 1997; Sederer and Summergrad, 1993).

Question Three. *What has been the fate of those mentally ill persons who are no longer served in state mental hospitals?*

In the past, "chronic mental patient" was considered to be acceptable terminology and was commonly used to refer to people who were enrolled in state mental hospitals (Bachrach, 1988a). In my 1976 monograph, I defined chronic mental patients as "those persons who are, have been, or might have been, but for the deinstitutionalization movement, on the rolls of state mental hospitals" (1976, p. 1). Today, sensitized to the distress that this term causes to many people who suffer from severe and persisting mental illnesses (Bachrach, 1992a, 1993b), I often attempt to substitute other language for this term. Yet, the definition I offered in 1976 precisely captures the focus of this third question. Apart from those individuals who might be enrolled in state mental hospitals on any given day, what has been the fate of this population?

Once again, there are no simple answers. Many of these persons have, according to a variety of outcome indices, been successfully treated in community-based service settings (Cohen, 1990; Dincin, 1995; Warner, 1995), although, as in the case of resident state hospital populations, percentages differ greatly among communities in accord with the variables discussed above. For these persons, the basic philosophy of deinstitutionalization—the notion that community care is more humane and more therapeutic than state mental hospital care (Bachrach, 1976)— is demonstrably valid, for the quality of their treatment and of their lives is vastly improved over that in state mental hospitals. Many of these individuals express much greater satisfaction with their life circumstances when those are contrasted with conditions inside the hospitals, and indeed some patients, in spite of their illnesses, have realized a certain degree of "normalization" in their daily activities. Some live independently and some are productively employed, achievements that were relatively rare in the days when state mental hospitals dominated our systems of care.

But these generalizations apply only to *some* mentally ill individuals. Other persons who might in the past have resided in state mental hospitals have been discharged to communities where there are few if any programs to serve them (Wong, 1997), and many end up living on the streets; others—an ever growing percentage of the total population of persons suffering from long-term mental illnesses—have never been admitted to state mental hospitals, nor any other treatment facilities, in the first place (Bachrach, 1978, 1992b), often as the result of so-called "admission diversion" policies (Geller, 1992)—sometimes little more than a euphemism for providing no care at all (Dionne, 1978; Sullivan, 1979).

Even in those places where community care has been thoughtfully conceived and adequately funded—even in service systems where great hope, effort, and clinical competence have been invested in community-based enterprises—some mentally ill persons are inadequately treated or entirely untreated (Dewees, Pulice, and McCormick, 1996). For example, some so-called "new chronic patients" have found it extremely difficult to sustain themselves in the community. Among other problems, their easy access to alcohol and other chemical substances has greatly exacerbated their psychiatric symptoms and interfered with any progress they might otherwise have made in community-based care (Bachrach, 1996a; Lamb and Shaner, 1993; Satel, 1996).

Somewhere between one-third and one-half of the nation's homeless individuals reportedly suffer from long-term mental illnesses (Lamb, Bachrach, and Kass, 1992). One recent estimate from Denver, Colorado, places the percentage at between 50 and 60 percent (Callahan, 1998). Many of these individuals would surely, in the past, have been served in state mental hospitals. Whether they are "better off" on the streets is a matter of personal judgment, although it is fair to say that at a minimum, their basic needs for food, shelter, clothing, and medical care would be met more readily within the hospital setting (Belkin, 1992).

Another significant portion of the population previously served in state mental hospitals can, as previously noted, be found in jails and other correctional facilities. Many of these individuals experience great difficulties in linking up with the mental health service system after their release.

How can we explain these disturbing circumstances in view of the early promise that community care held for mentally ill individuals? The plight of these underserved and unserved persons must in some part be attributed to such factors as community resistance to their integration into society, severe fragmentation in community-based service systems, and persistent funding problems (Bachrach, 1997; Bachrach and Lamb, 1989). Further complications doubtless arise from the fact that nothing in the world of mental health service planning stands still for long, a fact that makes it difficult to plan, justify, and sustain new programs. Old service structures disappear, and new service delivery practices are introduced, even as political support for improving mental health care in the nation grows increasingly uncertain (Bachrach 1991, 1997). Even the language of mental health service delivery changes dramatically in response to promises implied in "quick-fix" treatment concepts (Bachrach, 1994).

Thus, it is hardly surprising that state and local governments faced with the need to respond to a multitude of special interest groups have largely lacked the resources—and often, as well, the interest and will—to attend adequately to the needs of long-term mental patients (Kammer, 1995; Sowers, 1995; Wolpert, 1995). The irony in this situation is that now that we have considerable experience to guide us in future efforts to supplant state mental hospitals with alternative community-based facilities, we are faced with the reality that the care of mentally ill people is not merely a matter of social conscience and professional skill. It is also, unfortunately, very much a matter of politics and of changing service priorities. The idealism and hope of the 1960s—when community care was widely endorsed and aggressively pursued (and when funding seemed ever to be available)—has, at least temporarily, given way to more mundane considerations of cost containment in the design of mental health service systems (Bachrach, 1996b; Petrila, 1995; Pinheiro, 1998).

How then can we sum up the response to this third question? I would submit, first, that the fate of people no longer served in state mental hospitals has been so varied that it is difficult to make any summary judgment about their circumstances, or even about their whereabouts. Some have fared admirably; others have experienced living conditions at least as undesirable, and sometimes more life-threatening and inhumane, than what they might have known as state hospital residents. And although we now have considerable technology for improving the care of these underserved individuals—in the form of case-finding techniques, outreach and case management services, an array of residential opportunities, rehabilitation interventions, and specialized dual diagnosis programs (Carling, 1993; Cohen, 1990; Dincin, 1995; Warner, 1995; Zealberg, Santos, and Fisher, 1993)—their fate, given today's political climate and shrinking resources, is at best an embarrassment to the mental health community and society at large, and at worst an unqualified tragedy for them and their families.

Is it then time to reinstate our state mental hospitals as the central loci in our system of care? There is no clear-cut answer to this question, for it is largely a matter of judgment: one's own personal convictions must be considered. It is, however, important to note that on the one hand, the motives of those who call for a renaissance of state hospital care are often humane and should not be dismissed as necessarily reactionary (Dumont, 1995; Isaac and Jaffe, 1995; Lamb, 1992; Lamb and Shaner, 1993; Zaleski, Gale, and Winget, 1979). On the other hand, those who are disposed to view the cup of deinstitutionalization as being half full rather than half empty are for their part justified in fearing that a massive return to state hospital care at this juncture would undermine the slow but very real progress that we have made in building community-based mental health systems (Bachrach, 1997).

Both excellent and inferior treatment and care are found in both kinds of service settings, and neither can be described unqualifiedly as inherently better for all patients under all circumstances. Thus, efforts to reach productive coexistence are definitely in order at this time. It is important that we attempt once again, as we did during the early 1970s, to depolarize extreme views on the issue of state mental hospital care. People whose lives have been thwarted by severe mental illness must not be further victimized by the intransigence of ideologues or by the political correctness (Lamb, 1994; Wilson, 1993) of pragmatists.

Question Four. *What is an appropriate role for the state mental hospital in today's uncertain and rapidly changing systems of care?*

It is not sufficient to acknowledge that state mental hospitals continue to occupy a critical niche within the systems of care in many communities; we must go further and attempt to describe that niche even though this task is fraught with risks. Trying to outline the state mental hospital's proper place within the mental health system too often encourages us to play "geography games," in which the hospital is viewed as a collection of bricks and mortar and not as a facility—in some places the *only* facility—that provides specific services for mentally ill individuals.

The rules of geography games are not subtle; the winner is the person who supports any facility *other than* the state mental hospital, which, ideologically, is still widely viewed as inherently undesirable. Planners are, in fact, encouraged to play geography games whenever their programs are evaluated according to commonly used indices of hospital tenure—such as declines in numbers of admissions, resident patients, and length of stay—as outcome criteria. More subtle measures of appropriateness of services, quality of care, and quality of life (Bachrach, 1997; Kincheloe, 1997; Munetz and Geller, 1993) give the players in these games relatively few points.

Geography games are popular, partly because they simplify very complex events, and several steps must be taken to guard against their seductiveness. First, planners and service providers must acknowledge that despite the existence of model systems of community care in some selected American communities, the growth of community-based services in this country has thus far failed to eliminate the need for state mental hospitals (Kincheloe, 1997; van Norman and Stone, 1996). The issue, if one reads carefully between the lines in contributions to the literature, is not so much whether the community has the *potential* for providing a full array of services (Becker and Schulberg, 1976; Dincin and others, 1993; Okin, 1995) but rather whether it possesses the *resources* and the *will* to do so. Absent these critical ingredients, state hospital care must still be viewed as an essential element in any array of comprehensive services.

By focusing on service statistics as major outcome indices, geography games tend to discourage us from looking as closely as we might at what it is that state mental hospitals actually *do*. Thus, a second important step in guarding against those games is to assess the full array of services that these facilities provide (Bopp and Fisher, 1995; Munetz and Geller, 1993; Townsend and Seiden, 1987). The literature reveals that state mental hospitals actually fulfill an amazing array of functions. Not only do they typically monitor the course of illness among severely disabled individuals, but they also provide psychiatric treatment, medical care, rehabilitation, short- and long-term asylum, residential care, crisis intervention, social structure, and role definition (Bachrach, 1976, 1984; Kincheloe, 1997; Smith, 1998; Wasow, 1993). This is not to say that all hospitals necessarily render all of these services, nor even that they always offer the most desirable options. However, in many places state mental hospitals may well be the only facilities that provide even the most minimal care and asylum to persons in grave need of assistance. In those instances, it is the patients who are the real losers in geography games.

Furthermore, it is not solely patients who are served by state mental hospitals. For their relatives, the hospital may provide much needed respite and relief, as well as education and support (Craig and others, 1987). For the system of care, it may provide a venue where those individuals who appear to be most difficult to reach can be engaged in treatment. For the professional community, the hospital may afford unparalleled opportunities for research and training (Douglas and others, 1994; Miller, 1981). For society, it may serve as a place for segregating and confining dangerous individuals. And for local communities, particularly those located in rural areas, the state mental hospital may provide a tax base and a critical locus of employment.

This partial listing of state hospital functions (Bachrach, 1976) provides some clues to the proper role of those facilities in today's system of care in any particular community. Were the hospital merely a place for psychiatric and medical treatment, its functions could easily be supplanted by other short- or long-term treatment facilities in the community. Were it only a place of detention, its functions could readily be taken over by the criminal justice system. Were it merely a residential site for severely ill individuals, it could easily be replaced by an array of graded housing facilities. And although community-based agencies in some places have performed one or more, perhaps even all, of these functions with notable success, no single class of service entities has yet been able to match the state hospital for multifunctionality.

In summary, however well or poorly any individual hospital may execute the functions with which it has become identified—however inhumane the living conditions within it or however enlightened the treatment—there is a core of services whose specific content varies from place to place that still appears to belong to the state mental hospital. Recognizing this fact is not necessarily tantamount to endorsing the hospital's indefinite existence; it is merely a statement of reality. The British psychiatrist John Wing (1975) has eloquently summed up the concept by which the state mental hospital's role must be assessed:

> The quality of life lived by the patient and his relatives is the final criterion by which services must be judged. A good hospital is better than a poor hostel or a poor family environment. A good family environment is better than a poor hospital or a poor hostel. The same may be said of day-time environments—open employment, enclaves in ordinary commercial business, rehabilitation or sheltered workshops, or protected day centers. Universal denunciation of any one type of setting is likely to be harmful since it is clearly not based on rational principles of assessment, treatment or care [p. 254].

It is perhaps also relevant to mention—although I do so reluctantly, for I have never felt that cost should be the bottom line in planning services for those in need—that the downsizing of state mental hospitals has not uniformly resulted in cost savings (Hollingsworth and Sweeney, 1997; Okin, 1995), as so many early proponents of deinstitutionalization had anticipated, and as some service planners continue to assume today ("Help for the Mentally Ill," 1993; Swidler and Tauriello, 1995). In many instances, cost *shifting* may be a more accurate description of reality than cost savings (Kane, 1995), for the comprehensive care of severely disabled persons tends to be expensive no matter where it takes place; and as Thornicroft and Bebbington (1989) have noted, the more comprehensive and methodologically sophisticated a cost analysis is, the less certain it appears that community-based services are cheaper than those provided in mental hospitals.

Unified Systems of Care

All things considered, perhaps the time has come to reintroduce the notion of unified systems of care into our service planning efforts, particularly in this era of managed care when the execution of many state hospital functions has been severely threatened (Lazarus, 1994; Minkin, Stoline, and Sharfstein, 1994). Popular in the 1950s and 1960s, these initiatives, described by John Talbott (1983b) as "utopian," were ahead of their time: they proved to be too threatening to vested political interests, and they severely challenged established notions of appropriateness in resource allocation.

Are we more nearly ready to acknowledge their merits today? At least in theory, a unified system of care makes a proper assessment of the needs of all service users, enrolled or potential, in the catchment area (Glick, Klar, and Braff, 1984). Medical and psychiatric "necessity" is defined in the broadest possible way to include treatment, rehabilitation, and support service needs; and to the extent that it is feasible to do so, the collateral needs of persons other than patients—for example, family members—are also considered. However, the patient's welfare remains the central focus in the planning process.

Once levels of need have been assessed, the planning task becomes a matter of evaluating the availability of services for meeting those needs. Ideally, the state mental hospital should, like any other agency in the system of care, provide those services that it performs best, whether they fall into the realm of medical and psychiatric treatment, vocational training, day treatment, asylum care, or any other class of interventions. Duplication of services among agencies should be avoided whenever possible.

In this paradigm, it is essential that the state mental hospital not be considered a facility of last resort (Geller, 1991; Rachlin, Grossman, and Frankel, 1979; Spiro, 1982)—one where patients whom no other facility wants are "dumped"—but rather a full partner among agencies in the system of care (Rothbard and others, 1998). Appelbaum (1991) has aptly noted that in many instances, inferior care in state hospitals has become a self-fulfilling prophesy, because those facilities are unable to establish control over admission decisions and must accept as their lot whoever and whatever is handed to them. Including hospital representatives in systemwide planning meetings and communitywide case conferences, helpful mechanisms for ensuring interagency partnership and cooperation (Bachrach, 1993a) is too often overlooked and should be aggressively encouraged. Case management activities should not be confined to concerns affecting a single agency but should be systemwide, so that the case manager–patient relationship can flourish whether the individual is living in the hospital or in the community.

Utopian? Perhaps. Idealistic? Definitely. Essential? Decidedly. Practicable? Yes—but only with great effort and cooperation from the political powers that be. Talbott (1983a) clearly outlined the rationale for unified systems of care in 1983, and his reasoning makes a great deal of sense today, particularly with the growth of managed care ("Help for the Mentally Ill," 1993). Like Talbott, I hold hope for the future and believe, like him, that "states and regions, haltingly but steadily, will continue to move away from the current fragmentation of mental health services and toward coordination and integration, if not unification, of all services" (p. 111). This much we owe to those individuals who rely on our service systems for treatment, rehabilitation, support, and often basic survival.

References

Appelbaum, P. "Barring the State Hospital Door." *Hospital and Community Psychiatry,* 1991, *42* (4), 351–352.

Appleby, L., and others. "Length of Stay and Recidivism in Schizophrenia: A Study of Public Psychiatric Hospital Patients." *American Journal of Psychiatry,* 1993, *150* (1), 72–76.

Bachrach, L. *Deinstitutionalization: An Analytical Review and Sociological Perspective.* Rockville, Md.: National Institute of Mental Health, 1976.

Bachrach, L. "A Conceptual Approach to Deinstitutionalization." *Hospital and Community Psychiatry,* 1978, *29* (9), 573–578.

Bachrach, L. "Asylum and Chronically Ill Psychiatric Patients." *American Journal of Psychiatry,* 1984, *141* (8), 975–978.

Bachrach, L. "Deinstitutionalization: What Do the Numbers Mean?" *Hospital and Community Psychiatry,* 1986a, *37* (2), 118–119, 121.

Bachrach, L. "The Future of the State Mental Hospital." *Hospital and Community Psychiatry,* 1986b, *37* (5), 467–474.

Bachrach, L. "Defining Chronic Mental Illness: A Concept Paper." *Hospital and Community Psychiatry,* 1988a, *39* (4), 383–388.

Bachrach, L. "Transient Patients in a Western State Hospital." *Hospital and Community Psychiatry,* 1988b, *39* (2), 123–124.

Bachrach, L. "The 13th Principle." *Hospital and Community Psychiatry,* 1991, *42* (12), 1205–1206.

Bachrach, L. "'The Chronic Patient': In Search of a Title." *Hospital and Community Psychiatry,* 1992a, *43* (9), 867–868.

Bachrach, L. "What We Know About Homelessness Among Mentally Ill Persons: An Analytical Review and Commentary." *Hospital and Community Psychiatry,* 1992b, *43* (5), 453–464.

Bachrach, L. "Organizational Issues and Expertise in Care Innovation: Applying the Principles of Continuity of Care." In J. Wolf and J. van Weeghel (eds.), *Changing Community Psychiatry: Care Innovation for Persons with Long-Term Mental Illness in The Netherlands.* Utrecht: Netherlands Institute of Mental Health, 1993a.

Bachrach, L. "Should 'The Chronic Patient' Be Replaced? Reader Responses." *Hospital and Community Psychiatry,* 1993b, *44* (9), 817–818.

Bachrach, L. "The Semantics of Mental Health Service Delivery." Paper presented at the 47th annual meeting of the Ontario Psychiatric Association, Toronto, Jan. 28, 1994.

Bachrach, L. "Deinstitutionalization: Promises, Problems, and Prospects." In H. Knudsen and G. Thornicroft (eds.), *Mental Health Service Evaluation.* Cambridge, England: Cambridge University Press, 1996a

Bachrach, L . "Managed Care: Some 'Latent Functions.'" *Psychiatric Services,* 1996b, *47* (3), 243–244.

Bachrach, L. "Lessons from the American Experience in Providing Community-Based Services." In J. Leff (ed.), *Caring in the Community: Illusion or Reality?* Chichester, England: Wiley, 1997.

Bachrach, L., and Lamb, H. "What Have We Learned from Deinstitutionalization?" *Psychiatric Annals,* 1989, *19* (1), 12–21.

Becker, A., and Schulberg, H. "Phasing Out State Hospitals—a Psychiatric Dilemma." *New England Journal of Medicine,* 1976, *294* (5), 255–261.

Belkin, L. "Treating the Sick Can Mean Clothing Them Too." *New York Times,* Nov. 24, 1992, pp. B1–B2.

Bigelow, D., and others. "Characteristics of State Hospital Patients Who Are Hard to Place." *Hospital and Community Psychiatry,* 1988, *39* (2), 181–185.

Bopp, J., and Fisher, W. "The State Psychiatric Center as an Academically Affiliated Tertiary Care Hospital." *Psychiatric Quarterly,* 1995, *66* (3), 237–247.

Butterfield, F. "Prisons Replace Hospitals for the Nation's Mentally Ill." *New York Times,* Mar. 5, 1998, p. A1, p. A26.

Callahan, P. "Colorado Mentally Ill Count a Mystery." *Denver Post Online,* [http://www.denverpost.com]. Aug. 16, 1998.

Carling, P. "Housing and Supports for Persons with Mental Illness: Emerging Approaches to Research and Practice." *Hospital and Community Psychiatry,* 1993, *44* (4), 439–449.

Carr, A. "The Scary Situation in Our Shelters." *Washington Post,* Dec. 13, 1992, p. C8.

Casper, E. "Identifying Multiple Recidivists in a State Hospital Population." *Psychiatric Services,* 1995, 46 (10), 1074–1075.

Center for Mental Health Services. *Additions and Resident Patients at End of Year, State and County Mental Hospitals, by Age and Diagnosis, by State, United States, 1993.* Rockville Md.: Substance Abuse and Mental Health Services Administration, 1995a.

Center for Mental Health Services. *Double Jeopardy: Persons with Mental Illnesses in the Criminal Justice System: A Report to Congress.* Rockville Md.: Substance Abuse and Mental Health Services Administration, 1995b.

Cohen, N. (ed.). *Psychiatry Takes to the Streets.* New York: Guilford Press, 1990.

Craig, T., Goodman, M., Siegel, C., and Wanderling, J. "The Dynamics of Hospitalization in a Defined Population During Deinstitutionalization." *American Journal of Psychiatry,* 1984, *141* (6), 782–785.

Craig, T., and others. "Family Support Programs in a Regional Mental Health System." *Hospital and Community Psychiatry,* 1987, *38* (5), 459–460.

Dewees, M., Pulice, R., and McCormick, L. "Community Integration of Former State Hospital Patients: Outcomes of a Policy Shift in Vermont." *Psychiatric Services,* 1996, *47* (10), 1088–1092.

Dincin, J. (ed.). *A Pragmatic Approach to Psychiatric Rehabilitation: Lessons from Chicago's Thresholds Program.* New Directions for Mental Health Services, no. 68. San Francisco: Jossey-Bass, 1995.

Dincin, J., and others. "Impact of Assertive Community Treatment on the Use of State Hospital Inpatient Bed-Days." *Hospital and Community Psychiatry,* 1993, *44* (9), 833–838.

Dingman, P. "The Case for the State Mental Hospital." *Where Is My Home: Proceedings of a Conference on the Closing of State Mental Hospitals, Scottsdale, Arizona, February 14–15, 1974.* Menlo Park, Calif.: Stanford Research Institute, 1974.

Dinitz, S, and Beran, N. "Community Mental Health as a Boundaryless and Boundary-Busting System." *Journal of Health and Social Behavior,* 1971, *12* (1), 99–108.

Dionne, E. "Mental Patient Cutbacks Planned." *New York Times,* Dec. 8, 1978, p. B3.

Douglas, E., and others. "A Ten-Year Update of Administrative Relationships Between State Hospitals and Academic Psychiatry Departments." *Hospital and Community Psychiatry,* 1994, *45* (11), 1113–1116.

Dugger, C. "State Called Patient Violent, Then Let Him Roam." *New York Times,* Jan. 7, 1995, p. 1, p. 26.

Dumont, M. "Our Lady of the State Hospital." *Readings: A Journal of Reviews and Commentary in Mental Health,* 1995, *10* (4), 8–11.

Emery, E., Mitchell, K., and Lowe, P. "Records Show Mental Hospital Fails to Give Individualized Care." *Denver Post Online,* [http://www.denverpost.com]. Aug. 16, 1998.

Fisher, W., and others. "Case Mix in the 'Downsizing' State Hospitals." *Psychiatric Services,* 1996, *47* (3), 255–262.

Foderaro, L. "Mental Hospitals for Unwilling Gain Support in New York State." *New York Times,* June 17, 1994, p. A1, p. B4.

Freudenheim, M. "States Shelving Ambitious Plans on Health Care." *New York Times,* Jul. 2, 1995, p. 1, p. 20.

Friedrich, R., and Flory, C. "Is There Hope for Those Who Require Long-Term Care?" *Newsletter of the National Alliance for the Mentally Ill Advocate,* Mar.–Apr. 1996, p. 4.

Geller, J. "Rights, Wrongs, and the Dilemma of Coerced Community Treatment." *American Journal of Psychiatry,* 1986, *143* (10), 1259–1264.

Geller, J. "'Anyplace but the State Hospital': Examining Assumptions About the Benefits of Admission Diversion." *Hospital and Community Psychiatry,* 1991, *42* (2), 145–152.

Geller, J. "A Report on the 'Worst' State Hospital Recidivists in the U.S." *Hospital and Community Psychiatry,* 1992, *43* (9), 904–908.

Geller, J. "We Still Count Beds." *Psychiatric Services,* 1997, *48* (10), 1233.

Glick, I., Klar, H., and Braff, D. "Guidelines for Hospitalization of Chronic Psychiatric Patients." *Hospital and Community Psychiatry,* 1984, *35* (9), 934–936.

Goldstein, A. "St. Elizabeths Accreditation in Jeopardy." *Washington Post,* Apr. 2, 1997, p. B1, p. B7.

Harris, H. "Boiler Failure Limits Heat at St. Elizabeths." *Washington Post,* Dec. 12, 1995, p. E6.

Hayakawa, S. I. *Language in Thought and Action.* (3rd ed.) Orlando: Harcourt Brace, 1972.

"Help for the Mentally Ill." *New York Times,* July 3, 1993, p. 18.

Hollingsworth, E., and Sweeney, J. "Mental Health Expenditures for People with Severe Mental Illnesses." *Psychiatric Services,* 1997, *48* (4), 485–490.

Holohean, E., Banks, S., and Maddy, B. "Patient Subgroups in State Psychiatric Hospitals and Implications for Administration." *Hospital and Community Psychiatry,* 1993, *44* (10), 1002 1004.

Isaac, R. J., and Jaffe, D. J. "Mental Illness, Public Safety." *New York Times,* Dec. 23, 1995, p. 27.

Isaac, R., and Jaffe, D. "Committed to Help." *National Review,* Jan. 29, 1996, pp. 34–38.

Jaffe, D. "Change Involuntary Treatment Laws." *Newsletter of the National Alliance for the Mentally Ill Advocate,* Jan.–Feb. 1995, pp. 16–21.

Jones, M. "State Mental Hospitals: Demoralized, Forgotten?" *Hospital and Community Psychiatry,* 1978, *29* (9), 610.

Kammer, F. "Block Grants Will Worsen Poverty." *New York Times,* Aug. 1, 1995, p. A15.

Kane, C. "Deinstitutionalization and Managed Care: Déjà Vu?" *Psychiatric Services,* 1995, *46* (9), 883–889.

Kincheloe, M. "A State Mental Health System with No State Hospital: The Vermont Plan Ten Years Later." *Psychiatric Services,* 1997, *48* (8), 1078–1080.

Lamb, H. "Is It Time for a Moratorium on Deinstitutionalization?" *Hospital and Community Psychiatry,* 1992, *43* (7), 669.

Lamb, H. "Only Good News Is Politically Correct." *Hospital and Community Psychiatry,* 1994, *45* (6), 17.

Lamb, H. "The New State Mental Hospitals in the Community." *Psychiatric Services,* 1997, *48* (10), 1307.

Lamb, H., Bachrach, L., and Kass, F. (eds.). *Treating the Homeless Mentally Ill: A Report of the Task Force on the Homeless Mentally Ill.* Washington, D.C.: American Psychiatric Association, 1992.

Lamb, H., and Shaner, R. "When There Are Almost No State Hospital Beds Left." *Hospital and Community Psychiatry,* 1993, *44* (10), 973–976.

Lamb, H., and Weinberger, L. "Persons with Severe Mental Illness in Jails and Prisons: A Review." *Psychiatric Services,* 1998, *49* (4), 483–492.

Lazarus, A. "Managed Care: Lessons from Community Mental Health." *Psychiatric Services,* 1994, *45* (4), 301.

Lurigio, A., and Lewis, D. "Worlds That Fail: A Longitudinal Study of Urban Mental Patients." *Journal of Social Issues,* 1989, *45* (1), 79–90.

Lyons, J., and others. "Predicting Readmission to the Psychiatric Hospital in a Managed Care Environment: Implications for Quality Indicators." *American Journal of Psychiatry,* 1997, *154* (3), 337–340.

Miller, R. "Beyond the Old State Hospital: New Opportunities Ahead." *Hospital and Community Psychiatry,* 1981, *32* (1), 27–31.

Minkin, E., Stoline, A., and Sharfstein, S. "An Analysis of the Two-Class System of Care in Public and Private Psychiatric Hospitals." *Hospital and Community Psychiatry,* 1994, *45* (10), 975–977.

Munetz, M., and Geller J. "The Least Restrictive Alternative in the Postinstitutional Era." *Hospital and Community Psychiatry,* 1993, *44* (10), 967–973.

National Association of State Mental Health Program Directors. *Closing and Reorganizing State Psychiatric Hospitals: 1996.* State Mental Health Agency Profile System Highlights, no. 1. Alexandria, Va.: National Association of State Mental Health Program Directors, Dec. 1997.

"New Managers to Take Over Troubled Psychiatric Hospital." *New York Times,* Feb. 5, 1996, p. B5.

Okin, R. "Testing the Limits of Deinstitutionalization." *Psychiatric Services,* 1995, *46* (6), 569–574.

Ozarin, L. "State Hospitals as Acute Care Facilities." *Hospital and Community Psychiatry,* 1989, *40* (1), 5.

Petrila, J. D. "Who Will Pay for Involuntary Civil Commitment Under Capitated Managed Care? An Emerging Dilemma." *Psychiatric Services,* 1995, *46* (10), 1045–1048.

Pinheiro, M. V. "Dealing with Managed Care." [http://pw2.netcom/com/~mvp1/soloproviders1.htm]. Sep. 25, 1998.

Rachlin, S., Grossman, S., and Frankel, J. "Patients Without Communities: Whose Responsibility?" *Hospital and Community Psychiatry,* 1979, *30* (1), 37–39.

Redick, R., Witkin, M., Atay, J., and Manderscheid, R. *The Evolution and Expansion of Mental Health Care in the United States Between 1955 and 1990.* Mental Health Statistical Note, no. 210. Rockville, Md.: Substance Abuse and Mental Health Services Administration, 1994.

Rothbard, A., and others. "Cost Comparison of State Hospital and Community-Based Care for Seriously Mentally Ill Adults." *American Journal of Psychiatry,* 1998, *155* (4), 523–529.

Satel, S. "The Madness of Deinstitutionalization." *Wall Street Journal,* Feb. 20, 1996, p. A18.

Sederer, L., and Summergrad, P. "Criteria for Hospital Admission." *Hospital and Community Psychiatry,* 1993, *44* (2) 116–118.

Shapiro, J. "Patients Refused Admission to a Psychiatric Hospital." *Hospital and Community Psychiatry,* 1983, *34* (8), 733–736.

Smith, D., Jones, T., and Coye, J. "State Mental Health Institutions in the Next Decade: Illusions and Reality." *Hospital and Community Psychiatry,* 1977, *28* (8), 593–597.

Smith, R. "Implementing Psychosocial Rehabilitation with Long-Term Patients in a Public Psychiatric Hospital." *Psychiatric Services,* 1998, *49* (5), 593–595.
Sowers, W. "The Ethics of Public Sector Managed Care: Civic Responsibility or Malignant Neglect?" *Community Psychiatrist* (Newsletter of the American Association of Community Psychiatrists), summer 1995, pp. 1–2.
Spiro, H. "Reforming the State Hospital in a Unified System of Care." *Hospital and Community Psychiatry,* 1982, *33* (9), 722–728.
Stratas, N., Bernhardt, D., and Elwell, R. "The Future of the State Mental Hospital: Developing a Unified System of Care." *Hospital and Community Psychiatry,* 1977, *28* (8), 598–600.
Strauss, V. "As St. Elizabeths Crumbles, Many Advise Closing It." *Washington Post,* Jan. 23, 1996, p. A1, p. A5.
Sullivan, R. "Hospitals Will Gain by Cutting Bed Use." *New York Times,* Dec. 31, 1979, p. A1, p. A13.
Swidler, R., and Tauriello, J. "New York State's Community Mental Health Reinvestment Act." *Psychiatric Services,* 1995, *46* (5), 496–500.
Talbott, J. "The Future of Unified Mental Health Services." In J. Talbott, J. (ed.), *Unified Mental Health Systems: Utopia Unrealized.* New Directions for Mental Health Services, no. 18. San Francisco: Jossey-Bass, 1983a.
Talbott, J. (ed.). *Unified Mental Health Systems: Utopia Unrealized.* New Directions for Mental Health Services, no. 18. San Francisco: Jossey-Bass, 1983b.
Teplin, L. "The Prevalence of Severe Mental Disorder Among Male Urban Jail Detainees: Comparison with the Epidemiologic Catchment Area Program," *American Journal of Public Health,* 1990, *80* (6), 663–669.
Thompson, J., and others. "Changing Characteristics of Schizophrenic Patients Admitted to State Hospitals." *Hospital and Community Psychiatry,* 1993, *44* (3), 231–235.
Thornicroft, G., and Bebbington, P. "Deinstitutionalisation—from Hospital Closure to Service Development." *British Journal of Psychiatry,* 1989, *155* (1), 739–753.
Torrey, E. "Jails and Prisons—America's New Mental Hospitals." *American Journal of Public Health,* 1995, *85* (12), 1611–1613.
Townsend, E., and Seiden, M., "Structural Inefficiencies at a State Psychiatric Hospital." *Hospital and Community Psychiatry,* 1987, *38* (2), 127–129.
van Norman, J., and Stone, S. Letter to *Psychiatric Services,* 1996, *47* (8), 879.
Warner, R. (ed.). *Alternatives to the Hospital for Acute Psychiatric Treatment.* Washington, D.C.: American Psychiatric Press, 1995.
Wasow, M. "The Need for Asylum Revisited." *Hospital and Community Psychiatry,* 1993, *44* (3), 207–208, 222.
Wilson, W. "Response to Fred W. Becker's 'The Politics of Closing State Mental Hospitals.'" *Community Mental Health Journal,* 1993, *29* (2), 115–117.
Wines, M. "Mental Institutions May Be As Empty As They'll Ever Be." *New York Times,* Sep. 4, 1988, p. E6.
Wing, J. "Planning and Evaluating Services for Chronically Handicapped Psychiatric Patients in the United Kingdom." In L. Stein and M. Test (eds.), *Alternatives to Mental Hospital Treatment.* New York: Plenum, 1975.
Witkin, M., Atay, J., and Manderscheid, R. "Trends in State and County Mental Hospitals in the U.S. from 1970 to 1992." *Psychiatric Services,* 1996, *47* (10), 1079–1081.
Wolpert, J. "Scrooges Among Us." *Washington Post,* June 29, 1995, p. A21.
Wong, D. "Slow Exits at State Mental Hospitals: Recovering Patients Lack Places to Go." *Boston Globe Online,* [http://www.bostonglobe.com]. Mar. 3, 1997.
Zaleski, J., Gale, M., and Winget, C. "Extended Hospital Care as Treatment of Choice." *Hospital and Community Psychiatry,* 1979, *30* (6), 399–401.
Zealberg, J., Santos, A., and Fisher, R. "Benefits of Mobile Crisis Programs." *Hospital and Community Psychiatry,* 1993, *44* (1), 16–17.

LEONA L. BACHRACH *is associate dean of the William A. Keese School of Continuing Education, Asbury Methodist Village, Gaithersburg, Maryland. Since 1978, she has been a national and international consultant and lecturer on issues related to psychiatric service planning.*

Professionals who operate from a clinical rather than a political ethic must be prepared to reclaim and accept leadership roles and responsibilities, which have shifted to the political arena.

Public Policy and State Psychiatric Hospitals

Richard H. Hunter

The history of public institutions in America is tied to social policy and public attitudes toward "deviant" and dependent people. Prior to the 1820s, people who were defined as deviant, criminal, or otherwise physically or mentally dependent were not confined to public institutions. During the colonial period, people experiencing extreme poverty or mental illness stayed with relatives or neighbors. Criminals were fined or whipped, placed in stocks, or hanged. According to Rothman (1971, p. xiii) "They did not conceive of imprisoning them for specific periods of time."

Asylums

Beginning in the 1820s, the nation began constructing public institutions of various types (penitentiaries, almshouses, reformatories, and insane asylums) for the criminal, deviant, and dependent populations. There are several theories concerning the purpose of the institutions, but most agree that they were to promote the stability of society, to ensure cohesion of community, and to restore a necessary social balance. The early asylums were developed with a goal of providing *moral treatment* and proper guidance to people unable to properly adjust to society. The movement to encourage states to take responsibility for the care and treatment of people with psychiatric disabilities was propelled by the horrors uncovered in the workhouses and almshouses of the day and the successes reported by the superintendents of the original thirteen asylums. Moral treatment was receiving acclaim in both Europe and the United States as a humanitarian approach with outstanding success. It reached its height in America in the 1830s and 1840s. Moral treatment "assumed a close personal relationship between each patient and the superintendent of the asylum, which itself had to be small and to provide a pleasant environment. In this idyllic setting, internal restraints on behavior were sought and rewarded, idleness was frowned upon, and patients were treated as rational adults" (Johnson, 1990, pp. 6–7).

Important factors that permitted the early asylums to implement moral treatment were their small size and their ability to select who was admitted (Grob, 1973). This selection allowed them to admit people who clearly had mental illness, as opposed to the wide range of disorders that were later "assigned" to state hospitals. For many years, there was a belief that no asylum should ever exceed two hundred people. This led to heated arguments among the asylum superintendents and those wishing to expand the size of the asylums.

State Psychiatric Hospitals

In the mid-1800s, citing the successes of the early asylums, Dorothea Dix, of the Association of Medical Superintendents of American Institutions for the Insane (later to become the American Psychiatric Association), and others initiated campaigns to build state psychiatric hospitals for the ever growing population and to provide "moral treatments" to people residing (and suffering abuses) in the almshouses and workhouses. Co-occurring with the movement to build more psychiatric hospitals were a rapidly growing population and increased pressures to expand the size of the asylums and mental hospitals. As state hospitals were being built, their scope and mission were further ill defined and obscured by demands that they also serve paupers and people with mental retardation and physical disabilities of various types. Adding to the burden of early state hospitals was a rapidly growing immigrant population. Many immigrants experienced difficulty in adjusting and required admission to state hospitals, often creating major language barriers (Greenblatt, York, and Brown, 1955; Johnson, 1990; Bloom, 1977). Increasing population in the mental institutions, coupled with the prejudices regarding large numbers of foreign-born patients, led to the abandonment of moral treatment in American institutions.

After 1850, limiting admissions only to people with mental illness and limiting the number of admissions, thereby controlling the size of the institutions, were advantages not afforded the superintendents of state psychiatric hospitals. As a result, state hospitals were overwhelmed with the responsibility to house and care for the senile elderly, dependent people who were alcohol and drug addicted, people with all forms of mental illness and mental retardation, people with epilepsy, and people with dangerous behavior problems. According to Bloom (1977, p. 14), "Between 1845 and 1945 the United States saw the establishment of almost 300 state mental hospitals, nearly all of which—after an initial flurry of enthusiasm and hope—quickly lapsed into vast storehouses for some of the most disabled and miserable people in the country."

As the population aged, caring for the senile elderly became a major responsibility of the state hospitals (Grob, 1973, 1983). As a result of the State Care Act of 1890, most almshouses were closed by 1920, leaving the indigent elderly and senile with no place to go except the state hospitals. The responsibility for care of the senile elderly was not lifted from the state hospitals until the 1965 amendments to the Social Security Act creating Medicare and Medicaid. These amendments provided for federal payments for residential services (nursing homes) for the indigent elderly as long as the care was provided outside the state hospitals. These amendments created the nursing home industry as we know it today and allowed for the transfer of thousands of senile elderly people from state hospitals to nursing homes.

By 1955, the population of the state hospitals reached nearly 559,000 (Braddock, 1981). Overcrowding and underfunding overwhelmed public hospitals in nearly every state. State hospitals became a mechanism for social control in a rapidly growing nation with little time for or interest in the disadvantaged or unproductive. State and local governments were unwilling to allocate sufficient resources to provide an adequate level of care (Deutsch, 1948; Bloom, 1977). From almost the very beginning, state hospitals were not provided the chance to meet the reform goals of Dix and those advocating for humane care for the mentally ill.

During the 1940s, 1950s, and 1960s, there were a number of exposés that brought negative public attention to the plight of people living in the state hospitals. Books like Deutsch's *Shame of the States* (1948), Mary Jane Ward's novel *The Snake Pit* (1946), and Ken Kesey's novel *One Flew Over the Cuckoo's Nest* (1962) influenced public opinion about the bleak conditions in the nation's state hospitals. In 1961, Erving Goffman's book *Asylums* contributed both to the public's negative attitudes and to professional biases against mental hospitals, by the portrayal that negative symptoms of schizophrenia may be caused by the institutions themselves.

Deinstitutionalization

Deinstitutionalization was well under way prior to anyone planning for it or naming it (Johnson, 1990). The movement corresponded well to both the public interest and the political will of the times. States aggressively pursued the downsizing and closing of state hospitals as they pursued the relocation of people into any number of alternative settings under the auspices of mental health reform. Economics drove much of the *transinstitutionalization* of the elderly as states attempted to shift costs to the federal government, using Medicaid and Medicare benefits, by placing elderly people in nursing homes and other residential centers of various types. Deinstitutionalization roared through the 1970s and 1980s with little to stand in its way except a few thousand people who were too disturbed, too dangerous, or too disabled to adequately be served by nursing homes, private psychiatric hospitals, or community alternatives. In addition, many states diverted an increasing number of forensic patients and people identified as sexually dangerous from the corrections system into the state mental hospitals. From the mid-1970s to the mid-1980s, there was a redirection of patients to newly emerging community mental health initiatives.

As deinstitutionalization progressed, the residual population of state hospitals included people with mental illness and serious behavior disorders, forensic patients requiring court supervision, and people identified as sexually dangerous. Further, state hospitals increasingly served people who had difficulty adjusting to the community, who resisted taking needed medications, who used street drugs or alcohol to excess, and who periodically became violent. As these patterns of use suggest, the concept of social control for state hospitals became more clearly articulated. The ability to provide needed protection and control for a subset of severely disturbed individuals was, and still is, a necessary component of a comprehensive service network (see Bachrach, 1983).

Public policy concerning state hospitals continues to be unclear and inconsistent. Many states continue on their quest to close hospitals and are frustrated with the problems associated with providing cost-effective alternatives. After rating the states on their services to people with serious mental illness, Torrey, Erdman, Wolfe, and Flynn (1990) concluded, "Services for individuals with serious mental illness in the United States are a disaster by any measure used. Not since the 1820s have so many mentally ill individuals lived untreated in public shelters, on the streets, and in jails. Countless more live in substandard boarding homes or rundown transient hotels, or pass their lives watching television or smoking cigarettes because no rehabilitation services are available" (p. 1).

The "Torrey Report" provided extensive state-by-state analysis of both hospital and community programs for people with serious mental illness. The report concluded, "It is clear that whatever was supposed to happen did not happen and that deinstitutionalization was a disaster. . . . Services for people with serious mental illnesses in the United States in 1990 are the shame of the nation" (p. 4).

Political Control Versus Clinical Leadership

From the beginning, the asylums, and later the state hospitals, were run by medical superintendents. It was the primary role of the hospital superintendent to make daily rounds, to be involved with the patients, and to model the type of care to be provided in the hospital. In most states, this tradition lasted well into the 1970s, as most hospital superintendents and most state mental health commissioners were psychiatrists, psychologists, or other experienced mental health professionals. Beginning in the middle 1960s after the passage of Medicaid and Medicare, most states began a massive program to shift costs of treating dependent people from state funds to federal funds. Medicaid and Medicare allowed states to open the doors of state hospitals and discharge mostly elderly people to a rapidly developing for-profit nursing home industry. Minimal federal and state regulations allowed this health care industry to evolve using primarily a minimum-wage untrained workforce, with only the scant and often perfunctory involvement of professionally trained clinicians. Elderly and dependent people with mental illness or other brain disorders were placed under the care of these community facilities (institutions) with minimal access to nurses and physicians and practically no meaningful involvement with psychiatrists, psychologists, social workers, rehabilitation counselors, and other specialty clinicians employed by the state hospitals. High staff turnover and inadequate training of direct-care staff in these mostly private, for-profit, community settings plagued the industry from the very beginning and continue to affect the quality of care of our elderly and dependent citizens. This transinstitutionalization of our mentally ill elderly provided significant savings to state budgets due to federal cost sharing and expanded the complexity of the system. Further, it expanded the role of the state into licensing and oversight roles.

After the Community Mental Health Centers Construction Act of 1963 (CMHC Act, Title II of Public Law 88-164) and several subsequent amendments (1965, 1967, 1968, 1970, 1973, and 1975), most states began developing community mental health initiatives that further expanded the complexity of the system of services and further removed the state from direct services into oversight and management roles. As the complexity of the system grew, there was an ever increasing political involvement in the design and funding of emerging programs. The CMHC movement was led by different types of clinicians, not the physicians and psychiatrists who were historically in charge of the state hospitals. The shifting of resources from primarily state-funded to various federal cost-sharing arrangements and the promise of reducing the size and expenses associated with state hospitals led to more and more political involvement and control over the emerging service system. By the mid-1970s and beyond, more and more states began replacing clinical leaders (state commissioners, state hospital superintendents, mental health authority administrators) with politically oriented public administrators. The measure of quality of care began to rest more and more with outside accrediting-body surveys and less on the clinical experience and leadership of the mental health professionals running the system.

Despite the national attention and concern of two presidents (Kennedy and Carter), more political involvement at the state level generally meant more attention and concern for downsizing and closing state hospitals and managing costs of the emerging, partially state-assisted, community mental health programs. Stigma toward people with mental illness and mental retardation did not diminish much over the course of the last several decades, and state politicians rarely included mental health programs among their funding priorities.

In addition to the effects of stigma, economic constraints created pressures for many states during the 1970s and 1980s. Rising health care costs and recessions placed state budgets under severe strain, and mental health programs, especially if provided in state hospitals, were hard hit in many parts of the country. Continuing competition for funds between the favored community providers and the state hospitals, regardless of the quality of care either provided, allowed the politicians in many states to effectively ignore the needs of both systems. As more political control was exerted over state systems, clinical leaders were increasingly replaced by administrators who would carry out the will of the political leaders, often without regard to the impact on the quality of patient care.

A deputy commissioner once stated in a meeting of the state's facility directors, "Facility budgets are not based on quality and what is needed. Budgets are based on what the governor wants to give us, and the governor does not want to give mental health more money." A state mental health commissioner made the following statement to his entire executive staff, including all state hospital superintendents, when announcing the budget for the subsequent fiscal year:

> We should have gotten more [money] but the governor said it will not get better than this. Don't get trapped in any local group's efforts to increase the budget. It won't happen. Don't poor mouth this budget! Say only fantastic [explicative] things about this budget. Say only this is the best budget ever. Don't get trapped by the media. Work your union folks so they can see how great a budget this is. Tell them we should not see any facility closures for the next decade. Don't obsess about where we've been [significant downsizing]. Don't build controversy into this budget.

It was commonly known that avoiding facility closures for the next decade was not the true intent of the commissioners.

As more and more state hospitals replaced clinical superintendents with politically appointed administrators and states appointed commissioners from the ranks of political advocates, the quality of programming suffered. Not all state mental health systems were taken over by political machines, but those that were experienced an erosion of quality that directly resulted in increased suffering. A high-ranking official in a state commissioner's office once ordered hospital superintendents to lay off much needed direct-care staff and replace them with members of a labor union representing truck drivers. The union members were to be assigned to driving activity-therapy vans during the normal working hours (8 A.M. to 5 P.M.). In the evening, this task was to be performed by regular activity-therapy staff (to avoid excessive overtime costs). When questions were raised, it was announced that the governor had made a deal with that union for support in the upcoming election and that part of his promise was to create several new jobs for their members. It was further announced that any superintendent who opposed this directive would be fired.

This author recalls a conversation with a new mental health commissioner concerning that official's exchange with a prior commissioner who was a psychiatrist. The psychiatrist advised the new commissioner that his role was to protect the mental health department from the ill-advised influence of politicians and to resist patronage hiring and the allocation of money to programs based on political recommendations. The new commissioner proudly stated that he in no way intended to protect the system from political influence. He stated that "all decisions are political decisions" (obviously he was not an economist), and he fully *intended* to politicize the system. From then on, all executive appointments were made on a political basis, and the role of the appointees was to execute orders regardless of the cost or impact on patient care, to avoid (or cover) scandal, and to protect their political power base. Resource allocation decisions and facility downsizing and closure decisions were made based on political support rather than on improved system functioning and needs of patients. Slick public relations brochures and slogans replaced honest discussions of client needs and studies of system outcomes.

Policies and actions of the type described above show a failure of checks and balances between political power and social need. The result can be serious deterioration in the quality and integrity of services and immeasurable suffering for thousands of people with mental illness. System management and oversight can erode to the point at which clinical or patient-related decisions are routinely disregarded. Clinically inappropriate placement of patients to allow for the downsizing or closing of facilities or to otherwise reduce expenditures finds little resistance from administrators whose imperative is to protect their political power base rather than to advocate for patient needs. Large-scale transfers of psychiatric patients into nursing homes and other poorly funded residential programs allow for facility closures and downsizing, permitting resources to be redirected into more politically favored programs (schools, roads, prisons).

For example, recent investigative journalism has revealed that in Illinois, about twelve thousand people living in nursing homes have been diagnosed with mental illness and that dozens of nursing homes with the highest concentration of mentally ill patients have failed to meet even minimum standards (Berens, 1998a, p. 1). According to the *Chicago Tribune,* "It [Illinois] dumped thousands of mentally ill patients into nursing homes in order to collect Medicaid, which paid half the cost." Further, state workers "quietly reclassified" many to disguise the proportion who were mentally ill (Berens, 1998b, p. 13). Changing the diagnoses permitted the state to transfer funding responsibility to Medicaid. According to the *Tribune,* "The State of Illinois has improperly—and possibly illegally—collected an extra $50 million from Medicaid as part of an ongoing strategy to hide thousands of patients with mental illnesses inside nursing homes" (Berens, 1998d, p. 1). Among the alleged consequences of this social policy tragedy were gross undertreatment and mistreatment of people with serious psychiatric disabilities, hundreds of unnecessary assaults on fragile elderly people in the nursing homes (Berens, 1998c, p. 1), millions of dollars of profits made by politically powerful owners of nursing homes, and hundreds of thousands of dollars contributed to politicians in that state by the nursing home owners and their associations (Berens, 1998b).

The Future Role of State Hospitals

It is unlikely that the state hospitals of the future will have the luxury of selecting admissions and controlling their census as did the asylum superintendents of yesteryear. However, there have been advancements in both medical and psychological interventions that will permit outcomes to improve and surpass those reported during the era of moral treatment. Further, system enhancements, including the many community-based services and assertive community treatment programs, will ensure that people with milder forms of mental illness will not be totally dependent on hospitals as their primary provider of services. From the 1970s forward, there has been a proliferation of community service options that have demonstrated value for people with serious mental illness during various phases of the illness. Further, many of these initiatives dramatically reduce dependence on the public psychiatric hospitals for a substantial number of people. We are far beyond the point at which the state psychiatric hospital should reemerge as the center of care for people with mental illness. However, promises of the demise of the public mental hospital were shortsighted and were informed more by politics and personal conviction than by the realities of psychiatric illnesses, society's responsibility to provide for people with chronic and financially debilitating conditions, and the need for states to provide some measure of social control. The proper role of the state psychiatric hospital includes providing treatment, care, and protective services within a comprehensive system of care that includes a wide array of community services. This service array must include case management and assertive case management for people who frequently relapse, have difficulty taking necessary medications, use street drugs, or periodically become violent. In addition to a wide array of mental health services, physical health services, and vocational services, the community system must also attend to housing, transportation, and income support needs. The complexities of both the illness and the disabling nature of the disease require well-coordinated and integrated interventions that reach across service providers and are flexible to the various needs of individuals across their episodes of illness. The state psychiatric hospital is only one component of that service array, which becomes critically important only at certain times. The public mental hospitals can best function when their mission is well understood, when there are other less structured and protective short-term hospitals available, and when there is an adequate array of community supports.

The types of patients most likely to continue to require services in state hospitals include individuals who either do not respond well to medications or only respond partially, people who are behaviorally disordered and occasionally become violent, people who require intensive behavior programming, people who have a history of repeated violence or exhibit self-destructive tendencies, people who need to be taken off medications, people who are forensic patients, and people identified as sexually dangerous persons. The roles of social control and protection have become more clearly defined as a key responsibility of public mental hospitals.

Improved technology is available that will allow public mental hospitals to significantly enhance outcomes for patients. Advances in psychotropic medications, psychological and behavioral interventions, psychiatric rehabilitation, and instrumental and social skills programs have improved outcomes for many in public hospitals (Bedell, Hunter, and Corrigan, 1997; Corrigan and Yudofsky, 1996; Soreff, 1996; Hunter, 1995; Marsh, 1994; Paul and Menditto, 1992; Sullivan, Richardson, and Spaulding, 1991). However, to make the new technology work, the political and bureaucratic barriers must be overcome. This will require alliances among mental health professionals, provider agencies, consumers, and advocates. In addition, professionals who operate from a clinical rather than a political ethic must be prepared to reclaim and accept leadership roles and responsibilities, which have shifted to the political arena, and advocate for technology that will improve outcomes and quality of life of those in need of public hospital care.

References

Bachrach, L. "Planning Services for Chronically Mentally Ill Patients." *Bulletin of the Menninger Clinic,* 1983, *47* (2), 163–188.

Bedell, J., Hunter, R., and Corrigan, P. "Current Approaches to Assessment and Treatment of Persons with Serious Mental Illness." *Professional Psychology: Research and Practice,* 1997, *28* (3), 217–228.

Berens, M. J. "Dangerous Bedfellows." *Chicago Tribune,* Sept. 27, 1998a, p. 1.

Berens, M. J. "Mentally Ill 'Vanish'; A Windfall Appears." *Chicago Tribune,* Sept. 28, 1998b, p. 13.

Berens, M. J. "'Bed Brokers' Hit the Street." *Chicago Tribune,* Sept. 29, 1998c, p. 1.

Berens, M. J. "State Cashes in on Sham Diagnoses: Illinois Has Been Tampering with the Records to Disguise Mentally Ill Patients in Nursing Homes Across the State as Physically Ill, Thus Passing on a Portion of the Cost to Medicaid." *Chicago Tribune,* Oct. 28, 1998d, p. 1.

Bloom, B. *Community Mental Health: A General Introduction.* Pacific Grove, Calif.: Brooks/Cole, 1977.

Braddock, D. "Deinstitutionalization of the Retarded: Trends in Public Policy." *Hospital and Community Psychiatry,* 1981, *32* (9), 607–615.

Corrigan, P., and Yudofsky, S. (eds.) *Cognitive Rehabilitation for Neuropsychiatric Disorders.* Washington, D.C.: American Psychiatric Press, 1996.

Deutsch, A. *The Shame of the States.* Orlando: Harcourt Brace, 1948.

Goffman, E. *Asylums.* New York: Doubleday, 1961.

Greenblatt, M., York, R., and Brown, E. *From Custodial to Therapeutic Patient Care in Mental Hospitals: Explorations in Social Treatment.* New York: Russell Sage Foundation, 1955.

Grob, G. *Mental Institutions in America: Social Policy to 1875.* New York: Free Press, 1973.

Grob, G. *Mental Illness and American Society, 1875–1940.* Princeton, N.J.: Princeton University Press, 1983.

Hunter, R. "Benefits of Competency-Based Treatment Programs." *American Psychologist,* 1995, *50* (7), 509–513.

Johnson, A. *Out of Bedlam: The Truth About Deinstitutionalization.* New York: Basic Books, 1990.

Kesey, K. *One Flew Over the Cuckoo's Nest.* New York: Viking Penguin, 1962.

Marsh, D. (ed.). *New Directions in the Psychological Treatment of Serious Mental Illness.* New York: Praeger, 1994.

Paul, G., and Menditto, A. A. "Effectiveness of Inpatient Treatment Programs for Mentally Ill Adults in Public Psychiatric Facilities." *Applied and Preventive Psychology,* 1992, *1* (1), 41–63.

Rothman, D. *The Discovery of the Asylum.* New York: Little, Brown, 1971.

Soreff, S. (ed.). *Handbook for the Treatment of the Seriously Mentally Ill.* Seattle: Hogrefe & Huber, 1996.

Sullivan, M., Richardson, C., and Spaulding, W. "University-State Hospital Collaboration in an Inpatient Psychiatric Rehabilitation Program." *Community Mental Health Journal,* 1991, 27 (6),.441–453.

Torrey, E., Erdman, K., Wolfe, S., and Flynn, L. *Care of the Seriously Mentally Ill: A Rating of State Programs.* (3rd ed.) Washington, D.C.: Public Citizen Health Research Group and the National Alliance for the Mentally Ill, 1990.

Ward, M. *The Snake Pit.* New York: Random House, 1946.

RICHARD H. HUNTER is president of Clinical Outcomes Group, clinical associate professor in the Department of Psychiatry at the School of Medicine, Southern Illinois University, and a member of the American Psychological Association Task Force on Serious Mental Illness and Severe Emotional Disturbance.

We should be asking if individualized psychiatric rehabilitation services and technologies are being offered to the individual regardless of the setting in which that person resides.

State Hospitals in the New Millennium: Rehabilitating the "Not Ready for Rehab Players"

Paul Stuve, Anthony A. Menditto

The role of the state psychiatric hospital has changed during the course of the past century. Advances in psychopharmacology and in new and innovative community-based treatments have enabled many mentally ill individuals to live successfully in the community (Liberman, 1992), and the population of state hospitals is now but a fraction of what it once was (Witkin, Atay, and Manderscheid, 1996).

This exciting trend toward community integration and treatment has led some to speculate on the modern-day usefulness of state hospitals. Despite the fact that such facilities were involved in the psychosocial rehabilitation (PSR) movement from its beginnings (Paul and Menditto, 1992), community practitioners often express doubt that rehabilitation can even occur in inpatient settings and at times refer to state hospitals as "pits of despair" or "institutional dinosaurs" (Graham, 1996, pp. 2–3). In this narrow view, clients in state hospitals are said to receive some other "nonrehabilitation" type of service and are described, in the vernacular of community rehabilitation, as being "not rehabilitation-ready." It is a curious irony to find such stigmatizing language being used by practitioners of a movement known for its empowering and stigma-busting philosophy.

There is nothing in the accepted definitions of PSR (for example, Anthony and Liberman, 1992; Stockdill, 1985) that precludes its practice in inpatient settings. Thus, the concept of "rehabilitation readiness" seems misguided. Rather than asking if the mentally ill individual is ready to take advantage of rehabilitation services, we should be asking if individualized PSR services and technologies are being offered to the individual *regardless* of the setting in which that person resides. The simple truth is that *all* persons with mental illness are rehabilitation-ready, if only the appropriate rehabilitation tools would be extended to them. Thus, the rehabilitation-readiness concept is more appropriately applied to *institutions* or *organizations* than to *individuals*.

It is certainly possible to turn state hospitals into rehabilitation-ready facilities. However, simply because inpatient institutions *can* be made rehabilitation-ready, does it necessarily follow that they *should* be? Given the advances in community-based rehabilitation technology, many are asking why all clients cannot be treated in the community. The reason is, quite simply, that there exist subgroups of people with severe mental illnesses who still require the added supports, protection, and restrictiveness of state hospitals. Most notably, this population includes those individuals who are violent, highly symptomatic, or unable to care for themselves, as well as forensic clients committed to state hospitals by criminal courts. These "not ready for rehab players" are the target population of the rehab-ready state hospitals of the next millennium.

Making a state hospital rehabilitation-ready requires major changes (Paul, Stuve, and Cross, 1997). This applies not only to the treatment programs within the facility but also to the hospital's culture and philosophy, to the staff organizational hierarchy, to data and assessment systems, and to staff training and supervisory processes. Fulton State Hospital (FSH) in Missouri has spent the past decade making such changes. The process has brought with it many challenges and struggles, and in the course of changing FSH and in helping other state hospitals make similar changes, we have developed a number of strategies designed to keep the process moving forward.

Developing a Rehabilitation-Ready State Hospital Administration

At FSH, the hospital administration was largely rehab-ready when the changes began. They had become dissatisfied with conditions in the facility's maximum-security forensic center, where the population of severely mentally ill clients was growing as a result of increasing admissions and rehospitalizations with few discharges. Care in this unit was largely custodial in nature, and clients remained highly symptomatic and aggressive. Thus, the hospital administration formed a task force to review the literature and recommend alternative treatment approaches.

The task force identified the Social-Learning Program (SLP) (Paul and Lentz, 1977) as the treatment of choice for the target population, and the hospital administration conducted an aggressive recruitment initiative to hire SLP experts into clinical leadership positions. The administration then provided broad and extensive support to facilitate the initial implementation of the SLP in the maximum-security unit. Based on its success, the SLP was expanded to other inpatient wards as well as to on-campus group homes.

For many facilities, this type of administrative support does not exist at the outset. The impetus for change is sometimes forced by outside agencies via accreditation problems or lawsuits. The pressure to react with quick fixes is strong in many state systems and is made even stronger by the vulnerability of limited resources to rapid reallocation due to changes in the political landscape (see Hunter, Chapter Two). Under such conditions, gaining long-term commitment to changing a hospital's culture, philosophy, and service delivery system to a rehabilitation model is quite difficult.

Although the struggle to elicit and maintain administrative support for rehabilitation technologies is an ongoing one, it is imperative nonetheless. There must be systematic education of administrators and key decision makers about rehabilitation philosophy and principles, including exposure to outcome data from the literature and from other facilities that have implemented similar programs. Mental health officials can be surprisingly unaware of the empirical database for PSR programs. The credibility of in-house experts can be enhanced by obtaining expert consultation from outside the hospital. Rallying the support of advocacy groups such as local chapters of the National Alliance for the Mentally Ill, as well as external accrediting bodies, can also greatly enhance administrative support. Ideally, one or more key administrators will emerge as vocal advocates of the PSR model, helping promote the rehabilitation mission of the hospital and assuring that proper attention is paid to rehabilitation programming needs at the executive level.

Developing a Rehabilitation-Ready State Hospital Organizational Structure

When the SLP was brought to FSH, the organizational hierarchy that was in place was a centralized structure, quite common to state hospitals nationwide, based on *disciplinary departments*. Staff members were supervised primarily by their discipline head, who typically resided in an office in another part of the campus. This centralized organizational hierarchy is a primary obstacle to becoming a rehab-ready facility. Within such a structure, staffing decisions are generally made by supervisors having very little contact with the day-to-day operations of the ward to which the treatment professional is assigned. The needs of the overall treatment program are usually secondary in such staffing decisions. For example, a program manager attempting to add a skills-training group to the schedule of a particular staff member was likely to encounter resistance to changing the status quo duties, both from the staff member and the supervisor. With primary supervisory authority lying so far away from the actual treatment team, the program manager was reduced largely to the role of "cheerleader" in an effort to organize effective programs and treatment teams.

At FSH, this discipline-based centralized hierarchy was replaced with a decentralized, interdisciplinary rehabilitation model for the initial SLP ward. A *team leader* was given final decision-making authority on treatment schedules and direct-care staff responsibilities. Thus, with primary supervisory responsibility and authority over the SLP social worker, psychologist, occupational therapist, special education teacher, recreation staff, and nursing staff, the team leader is able to better integrate staff into the treatment team and make any scheduling adjustments necessary to meet the needs of the program. In addition, direct performance-based feedback is possible, which is often not the case with a centralized model in which supervisors are far removed from the actual treatment setting. Finally, disciplinary action can be taken by the team leader as necessary.

This shift in management organization resulted in a number of challenges. Some staff opposed the development of program-based lines of authority and supervision, preferring instead to retain an exclusively discipline-based centralized model. Thus, the shift occurred slowly over several years, at times causing confusion and even dissension among line staff, managers, and supervisors. Nevertheless, with the strong support of hospital administration, and as staff became accustomed to the change, the new model was implemented on other SLP wards as they were developed. It is now the supervisory model hospitalwide.

Implementing Rehabilitation Technologies in the State Hospital

The SLP at FSH is designed to meet the rehabilitation needs of severely mentally ill clients with multiple skills deficits who require extended inpatient care. It is based on the empirically validated premise (Paul and Lentz, 1977) that no matter how severely impaired, mentally ill persons can and do learn. The SLP provides an environment to foster and maximize such learning. It is an integrated network of learning-based techniques and skills-training technologies comprehensively applied by all staff, across all waking hours, for all problem areas. Emphasis is placed on decreasing bizarre, unusual, and aggressive behaviors and on improving self-care skills, problem-solving and social skills, and vocational and leisure-time skills. All of this is structured around a *token economy system,* which greatly facilitates operant-based learning of the component behaviors that constitute various skill areas. Within this structure are individual, small group, and unit-wide interventions that target self-care skills, interpersonal and communication skills, cognitive functioning, leisure skills, medication and symptom management, academic skills, community awareness, and vocational skills. As clients meet treatment goals, they progress through a series of program steps with increasing responsibilities and privileges on their way to discharge.

A number of treatment techniques are used routinely throughout the SLP by all staff involved in providing direct care to clients, and staff usage of these techniques is monitored regularly through direct observation to assure that they occur with the proper frequency and in the proper context on the ward. A core tenet of the program is that all interactions between staff and clients have the potential to be therapeutic. Staff are expected to deliver high rates of verbal and nonverbal praise in response to appropriate client behavior, thus reinforcing these behaviors and encouraging their continued occurrence. Development of new adaptive behaviors is accomplished through modeling and direct instruction. Prompting is sometimes necessary to encourage clients to do things that they have the skills to do but do not always do spontaneously. Prompting always specifies the reasons for engaging in a certain behavior, so that clients develop a clear understanding of the impact their behavior has on their ultimate goals. Thus, instead of saying, "Bob, it's time to go to class," staff would say, "Bob, let's go to class now. We're going to be talking about ways to find fun things to do in the community, and that's going to be really helpful for you when you are discharged." In this fashion, Bob understands that going to class is important not because staff told him to go but because attending class has important consequences for Bob's ultimate goal of living in the community.

Shaping procedures are a very important part of SLP technology and are essential to teaching behaviors and skills to severely impaired clients (Menditto, Baldwin, O'Neal, and Beck, 1991). This consists of breaking down a behavior into smaller component behaviors and reinforcing successive approximations. Target behaviors are made progressively more difficult by increasing the amount of time that must be spent on the task or by increasing the complexity of the task. Reinforcement consists of verbal and nonverbal praise, snacks, and tokens that can be redeemed in the ward token store for a variety of consumables or privileges. The skills that are targeted by the SLP shaping classes include on-task participation in groups, personal-grooming tasks, and appropriate social interaction skills.

The SLP also uses a number of techniques designed to help clients decrease maladaptive behaviors and substitute more appropriate and adaptive behaviors. Extinction procedures and differential reinforcement of other behaviors are used to decrease behaviors that are bizarre, overly intrusive, or otherwise incompatible with successful community living. Substantial effort is directed toward assuring that clients receive attention for appropriate and adaptive behaviors and not for maladaptive behaviors. For example, staff at custodial and non-rehab-ready facilities routinely ignore clients who are sitting quietly in the dayroom and provide attention only when clients are behaving in a disruptive or bizarre manner. In the SLP, sitting quietly in the dayroom is an opportunity for staff to engage in appropriate conversation with a client, whereas bizarre or mildly disruptive behaviors are ignored as much as possible. As clients learn that appropriate and adaptive behaviors are the ones that are reinforced and maladaptive behaviors are not, the latter decrease in frequency and are replaced with the adaptive behaviors that will be necessary for successful community living.

For some maladaptive behaviors, however, it is impossible or inadvisable to ignore them. Behaviors that are unacceptable in society are targeted by a number of SLP techniques designed to help clients act responsibly, fairly, and safely. Thus, whereas stealing, harassing others, and threatening or assaultive behaviors are discouraged by laws and fines in the real world, the SLP addresses such acts through program rules and by response costs in the form of token fines. For example, stealing from another client results in a fine of ten tokens, but assaults carry a fine of twenty-five tokens—virtually an entire day's worth of token earnings.

Clients who engage in frequent aggressive behaviors pose particular challenges to state hospitals. Threatening and assaultive behaviors are among the most obvious indicators of potential risk of harm to self or others and can very quickly result in readmission to state hospitals. Effective treatment of these behaviors is essential if subsequent community placements are to succeed. We have treated a large number of seriously assaultive clients in our maximum-security forensic setting and have found that a combination of the SLP and pharmacotherapeutic interventions offer the best success in addressing such behaviors (Beck and others, 1991; Menditto and others, 1996; Menditto, Beck, and Stuve, in press).

Developing Rehabilitation-Ready Data Systems in the State Hospital

The PSR movement prides itself on the use of assessment data to guide the development, implementation, and evaluation of individualized interventions and emphasizes the use of aggregate data to evaluate program processes and outcomes. Perhaps more than any other PSR strategy, the SLP is data driven, with data collection geared toward providing a wide array of stakeholders with the information they need for effective decision making. Bringing the SLP to FSH included implementation of the Staff-Resident Interaction Chronograph (SRIC) (Paul, 1987a) and the Time-Sample Behavioral Checklist (TSBC) (Paul, 1987b). Data for these systems are gathered according to stratified hourly time sampling by a team of noninteractive observers, providing objective measures of the nature of staff activity and staff-client interactions and detailed level-of-functioning information on clients in the SLP. Reliability for these instruments is maintained at .95 or above.

SRIC data are gathered from observations of staff made during performance of their everyday program responsibilities. A single SRIC round collects information on the nature of all staff behaviors and interactions with clients for a period of ten consecutive minutes. For each staff-client interaction occurring within this time frame, observers record the type of behavior the client is engaging in (for example, appropriate, inappropriate, neutral) and the type of response that the staff member provides to that behavior (for example, verbal praise, prompt, ignore, and so forth). All direct-care staff, from psychiatric aides to senior-level clinicians, are observed in this fashion at a frequency of about one to five times per week, depending on the amount of time typically spent on the ward by the particular staff member. Data are entered into the computer, and reports are prepared that provide detailed information on the nature and rate of staff behavior, both individually and in aggregate form.

TSBC data are collected from observations of clients made at preselected times during their everyday ward routine and scheduled groups and activities. Information is recorded on the client's location, social orientation, and facial expression, as well as on the occurrence of a number of appropriate behaviors (such as talking or listening to others, participating in group activities, or playing a game), inappropriate behaviors (such as talking to oneself, discussing patently delusional material, or exhibiting threatening or assaultive behaviors), and unusual motor behaviors (such as tremors, stereotypical movements, or pacing). There are a total of seventy-four of these observational codes, and they can be grouped into seven "higher-order" categories, including, for example, broad indices for interpersonal interaction, unusual psychomotor behaviors, and hostility. Each client is observed eighty to a hundred times each week. These data are entered into the computer, and weekly reports and graphs are prepared for each patient.

A third assessment system in place in the SLP at FSH is the Clinical Frequencies Recording System (CFRS) (Redfield, 1979). This system consists of a variety of data on client attendance and participation in scheduled groups and treatment activities, performance of routine grooming and hygiene tasks, assorted low-frequency but critical problem behaviors exhibited on the ward (for example, assaults), and the type and frequency of reinforcers accessed by the client (for example, grounds passes, snacks, TV privileges). Additional staffing is not necessary for the CFRS; these essential data are routinely collected throughout the day by all direct-care staff having contact with clients for purposes of treatment. All relevant information is gathered by use of event recording on simple forms that take from a few seconds to only a couple of minutes to complete. These data are then entered into the computer database by night-shift staff at the end of each day.

Data from these three assessment systems are assembled in reports that meet the needs of all stakeholders within the rehab-ready state hospital as well as external stakeholders such as accrediting bodies, families, and advocacy groups. Data on client functioning are shared with individual clients to show progress over time and are used to get baseline measures and to examine weekly changes in functioning and to select, evaluate, and modify treatment targets and goals. The impact of a social skills class may be evaluated by looking at information on class participation provided by the CFRS as well as at changes in a number of social-functioning behaviors measured by the TSBC. Similarly, the TSBC is especially useful in spotting increases or decreases in psychotic behaviors and motor side effects as a result of medication changes. Thus, data from these instruments guide decision making regarding new rehabilitation and pharmacotherapeutic interventions.

Information on staff who provide direct services is of particular interest to supervisors and program managers seeking data on overall staff effort and workloads as well as adherence to SLP principles and procedures. The SRIC can provide data on appropriate staff interactions (for example, providing verbal praise to a client who is successfully participating in a social skills group) as well as inappropriate staff interactions (for example, ignoring a reasonable request from a client) on both an individual and a ward-wide basis. The CFRS can report information on the number of treatment hours and client-contact hours provided by a staff member for a given time period. Thus, managers receive objective data for use in providing individual feedback on job performance as well as making determinations about overall staff-training needs.

Aggregate and longitudinal data provided by these systems are used for quality improvement purposes, program evaluation, and outcome research, permitting comparisons between multiple wards and programs, examination of interactions among two or more interventions, and evaluation of the impact of training procedures. We have published a number of studies that have made use of such data (for example, Beck and others, 1997; Finnell, Card, and Menditto, 1997; Menditto and others, 1996; Pestle, Card, and Menditto, 1998).

Finally, data are also readily available to answer questions of outside accrediting agencies. Surveyors are particularly impressed by the ready availability of such quality data and by the ongoing nature of the data collection systems.

The commitment to starting up these systems is not small. Although the CFRS is implemented by existing ward staff as part of their regular clinical duties, the TSBC and SRIC require a team of four or five observers per two wards, plus one additional observer supervisor for every three to four wards. At FSH, the original observer positions were created without allocating any additional funds by converting vacant clerical and nursing positions at the hospital.

A second consideration is the fair amount of resentment some staff display in response to having their job performance so closely monitored on such a regular basis. At FSH, many staff initially expressed concern that the SRIC data were only being gathered in order to "get" staff and were unwilling to consider the positive aspects that such data provide in terms of staff development and training, enhancement of skills, and the like. In our experience, explanations of these benefits are not enough to allay staff members' fears; this occurs only after the actual systems are in place, and staff members can see for themselves how the data are being used. Since its implementation, staff have received positive SRIC-based feedback (both verbal and written) at a rate that outweighs negative feedback by a substantial margin. This has gone a long way toward reducing initial resistance to the SRIC.

At FSH, the financial costs of the TSBC and SRIC systems, as well as the supervisory efforts necessary to overcome initial staff resistance, have been more than offset by the detailed level of individualized clinical interventions, increased productivity and effectiveness of staff, and ongoing availability of program evaluation data that result from their use (Menditto, Valdes, and Beck, 1994; Paul, 1986). The systems are so successful, in fact, that FSH currently has them implemented on a total of ten wards.

Training and Maintaining a Rehabilitation-Ready Staff

Another challenge in implementing the SLP at FSH involved adjusting the ways staff think about and behave toward clients. Nursing staff in particular were required to shift from a caretaker role and the "doing for" mentality common in non-rehab-ready facilities to the role of guide and teacher and a "doing with" mentality, which is necessary in a rehabilitation setting. A shift required of professional-level staff has been a move away from more traditional office-based psychotherapy orientations to a more ward-based, in vivo, skills-training approach.

These changes have met with resistance from staff who prefer the more traditional roles. Resolution to such resistance has come from the SLP's heavy emphasis on staff training and reorientation not only prior to implementation but also on an ongoing basis. Training must be especially sensitive to the need for changes in long-standing roles and beliefs. Most staff have adapted and flourished in these new roles, although some have chosen to leave the hospital in order to continue practicing in more traditionally oriented settings.

Making the Forensic State Hospital Rehabilitation-Ready

Turning a forensic center into a rehabilitation-ready setting brings with it special challenges. At FSH, a number of issues had to be addressed to permit implementation of the SLP in our maximum-security forensic center. The largest obstacle was undoubtedly the custodial and penal atmosphere of the forensic center. Patients essentially "did time," while receiving very traditional therapies from mental health professionals. Psychiatric aides functioned first and foremost to keep the peace and maintain order on the wards, and secondarily as nursing assistants. Many staff opposed the implementation of the SLP and its shift toward a more rehabilitation-oriented philosophy in this setting, expressing skepticism that treatment and security could coexist.

Thus, in addition to the extensive training and supervision issues discussed above, other changes and modifications to the SLP had to be made to permit its operation in a maximum-security setting. For example, unlike the original SLP described in Paul and Lentz (1977), maximum-security forensic clients could not be allowed passes or skills training and generalization activities outside the building. Vocational training opportunities had to be limited to those utilizing materials that met building security codes. Family style dining involving clients and staff—an important normalizing experience of the original SLP—was not included in the forensic SLP due to the security precautions necessary in the centralized dining area. In addition, new skills-training and reeducative groups had to be developed to address criminal behavior patterns.

These changes required for our maximum-security setting have worked quite well, and the modified SLP has been able to address a wide range of client needs while coexisting with the unit's necessary security procedures (Menditto, Valdes, and Beck, 1994). Nevertheless, these modifications have limited somewhat the SLP's full rehabilitation potential. Eventually, it became apparent that changes to FSH's other forensic unit would be necessary in order that clients moving from maximum-security to minimum-security wards could continue to be involved in rehabilitation programming. The SLP was therefore expanded to include a ward within FSH's minimum-security facility. On this less restrictive ward, clients are able to take grounds passes, participate in rehabilitation activities in the community, and enjoy a more complete range of vocational-training opportunities.

Eventually, the issue of discharge arose. Discharge from an inpatient setting is difficult for clients with long lengths of stay and is especially so for clients with forensic histories. For community providers, accepting clients with histories of brutal crimes is generally not a high priority. For clients, the transition from a setting that has been "home" for years in many cases is very anxiety provoking. Once a client has been accepted to a community facility, a gradual transition back into the community is often indicated. Ideally, this would consist of initially brief visits to the discharge setting, followed by a gradual progression to longer day visits, overnight stays, several-night stays, and finally discharge. This kind of flexible transitioning, which may take several weeks, is difficult to accomplish in privately run group homes, most of which have waiting lists and fiscal considerations that require immediate filling of vacancies. Therefore, FSH initially converted a staff residence into a group home to permit such discharge flexibility. Residents of the group home—which is located on the edge of the hospital grounds adjacent to the Fulton community—continue to receive treatment according to social-learning principles, although a more intensive focus was provided for those skills necessary for independent community living. Clients plan and prepare their own meals, work at either the local sheltered workshop or in supported-employment jobs, take care of their own housekeeping and yard chores, and enjoy recreational, social, and leisure activities in the community.

Maintaining the rehabilitation-ready status of a forensic hospital is an ongoing struggle. The very nature of the forensic population invites the critical vigilance of the media and at times provokes involvement from legislatures and other nonclinical entities. In Missouri, the negative media attention received in the aftermath of three recent forensic elopements has resulted in a number of changes to our forensic system. This has included the addition of a medium-security level to the state's already existing maximum- and minimum-security levels, a more detailed forensic review process prior to considering discharge, and increased scrutiny of all patients (even nonforensic ones) before granting privileges. At FSH, nonforensic beds have been reduced in order to make room for the intermediate security unit.

Such changes can distract rehabilitation-ready facilities from their primary treatment mission. New policies and procedures developed out of such circumstances are often quite restrictive and can have the unwanted side effect of depriving patients of access to certain rehabilitation interventions, especially those related to community reintegration. Although the nature of the forensic population merits extra caution, care is nevertheless required to assure that new policies and procedures truly protect the public interest and safety and are not merely examples of "cracking down" on embarrassing situations. Research can help guide the application of new policies and procedures to assure that the resulting restrictions are not indiscriminately applied to patients who pose only minor risks as well as to those posing major risks (Menditto,

Linhorst, Beck, and Stuve, 1999). As the number of forensic beds continues to expand nationwide, the rehabilitation-ready facility must be prepared to carefully examine and balance issues of security, safety, and reasonable access to rehabilitation interventions, lest we create a new generation of back-ward environments for society's latest group of "undesirables."

Summary

Over the past ten years, FSH has seen the initial implementation of the SLP grow from a single ward in the maximum-security forensic unit to include three additional wards within that unit, two wards on the medium-security forensic unit, and two wards within the general adult psychiatric service. There are now four FSH group homes, which admit clients from the hospital's forensic as well as nonforensic populations. Six to eight clients live in each home and function in a relatively self-sufficient manner, and many more (including forensic clients) have been discharged from the group homes and now live independently in the community. They work in supported employment or competitive job settings and manage their own households. Several of our discharged clients even return to visit us from time to time.

The FSH administration remains solidly committed to being a rehabilitation-ready facility. We have had a number of positive outcomes over the years (Baldwin and others, 1992; Beck and others, 1991; Beck and others, 1997; Finnell, Card, and Menditto, 1997; Menditto, Baldwin, O'Neal, and Beck, 1991; Menditto, Valdes, and Beck, 1994; Menditto and others, 1996; Menditto, Beck, and Stuve, in press; Pestle, Card, and Menditto, 1998), and we regularly host visitors from other state hospitals seeking consultation on how to make their own facilities rehabilitation-ready. Recently, we were featured on a segment of the nationally broadcast medical education program *psychLINK* (Glazer, 1998), where it was suggested that rehabilitation programming models such as ours represent the future of state hospitals. The "Not Ready for Rehab Players" think so too.

References

Anthony, W., and Liberman, R. "Principles and Practice of Psychiatric Rehabilitation." In R. Liberman (ed.), *Handbook of Psychiatric Rehabilitation.* Old Tappan, N.J.: Macmillan, 1992.

Baldwin, L., and others. "Decreasing Excessive Water Drinking by Chronic Mentally Ill Forensic Patients." *Hospital and Community Psychiatry,* 1992, *43,* 507–509.

Beck, N., and others. "Reduced Frequency of Aggressive Behavior in Forensic Patients in a Social Learning Program." *Hospital and Community Psychiatry,* 1991, *42,* 750–752.

Beck, N., and others. "Risperidone in the Management of Violent, Treatment-Resistant Schizophrenics Hospitalized in a Maximum Security Forensic Facility." *Journal of the American Academy of Psychiatry and the Law,* 1997, *25,* 461–468.

Finnell, A., Card, J., and Menditto, A. A. "A Comparison of Appropriate Behavior Scores of Residents with Chronic Schizophrenia Participating in Therapeutic Recreation Services and Vocational Rehabilitation Services." *Therapeutic Recreation Journal,* 1997, *31,* 10–21.

Glazer, W. "Violence and Aggression: Breaking the Cycle." *PsychLINK.* (Television broadcast.) Gaithersburg, Md.: Interactive Medical Networks, 1998.

Graham, S. "President's Message." *International Association for Psychosocial Rehabilitation Services (IAPSRS) PSR Connection Newsletter,* 1996, Issue 3, pp. 2–3.

Liberman, R. (ed.). *Handbook of Psychiatric Rehabilitation.* Old Tappan, N.J.: Macmillan, 1992.

Menditto, A. A., Baldwin, L., O'Neal, L., and Beck, N. "Social-Learning Procedures for Increasing Attention and Improving Basic Skills in Severely Regressed Institutionalized Patients." *Journal of Behavior Therapy and Experimental Psychiatry,* 1991, *22,* 265–269.

Menditto, A. A., Beck, N., and Stuve, P. "A Social-Learning Approach to Reducing Aggressive Behavior Among Chronically Hospitalized Psychiatric Patients." In M. Crowner and L. Burney (eds.), *Understanding and Treating Aggressive Psychiatric Patients.* Washington, D.C.: American Psychiatric Press, in press.

Menditto, A. A., Linhorst, D., Beck, N., and Stuve, P. *Predicting Elopements Among Psychiatric Patients with a Special Emphasis on Those Committed for Violent Criminal Offenses.* Manuscript in preparation, 1999.

Menditto, A. A., Valdes, L., and Beck, N. "Implementing a Comprehensive Social-learning Program Within the Forensic Service of Fulton State Hospital." In P. Corrigan and R. Liberman (eds.), *Behavior Therapy in Psychiatric Hospitals.* New York: Springer, 1994.

Menditto, A. A., and others. "Effectiveness of Clozapine and a Social Learning Program for Severely Disabled Psychiatric Inpatients." *Psychiatric Services,* 1996, *47,* 46–51.

Paul, G. (ed.). *Assessment in Residential Treatment Settings: Principles and Methods to Support Cost-Effective Quality Operations.* Champaign, Ill.: Research Press, 1986.

Paul, G. (ed.). *The Staff-Resident Interaction Chronograph.* Champaign, Ill.: Research Press, 1987a.

Paul, G. (ed.). *The Time-Sample Behavioral Checklist.* Champaign, Ill.: Research Press, 1987b.

Paul, G., and Lentz, R. *Psychosocial Treatment of Chronic Mental Patients: Milieu Versus Social-Learning Programs.* Cambridge, Mass.: Harvard University Press, 1977.

Paul, G., and Menditto, A. A. "Effectiveness of Inpatient Treatment Programs for Mentally Ill Adults in Public Psychiatric Facilities." *Applied and Preventive Psychology,* 1992, *1* (1), 41–63.

Paul, G., Stuve, P., and Cross, J. "Real-World Inpatient Programs: Shedding Some Light—a Critique." *Applied and Preventive Psychology,* 1997, *6,* 193–204.

Pestle, K., Card, J., and Menditto, A. A. "Therapeutic Recreation in a Social-Learning Program: Effect Over Time on Appropriate Behaviors of Residents with Schizophrenia." *Therapeutic Recreation Journal,* 1998, *32,* 28–41.

Redfield, J. "Clinical Frequencies Recording Systems: Standardizing Staff Observations by Event Recordings." *Journal of Behavioral Assessment,* 1979, *1,* 211–219.

Stockdill, J. (1985). *Definition of Psychosocial Rehabilitation.* Technical Assistance Transmittal No. 1—National Institute of Mental Health Office of State and Community Liaison to State Mental Health Directors. Rockville, Md.: National Institute of Mental Health, 1985.

Witkin, M., Atay, J., and Manderscheid, R. "Trends in State and County Mental Hospitals in the U.S. from 1970 to 1992." *Psychiatric Services,* 1996, *47* (10) 1079–1081.

PAUL STUVE is program coordinator for psychosocial rehabilitation services in Fulton State Hospital's adult psychiatric unit and clinical assistant professor in the Department of Psychiatry and Neurology at the School of Medicine, University of Missouri.

ANTHONY A. MENDITTO is director of psychosocial rehabilitation services at Fulton State Hospital and clinical assistant professor in the Department of Psychiatry and Neurology at the School of Medicine, University of Missouri.

Ultimately, the outcome and cost-effectiveness research should convince a compassionate public that rehabilitation is worthwhile, wherever it takes place.

The Unique Roles of State Hospital Programs: Keeping What Works in an Evolving System

Mary Sullivan

This chapter is a case study of changes in a mental health system. Its purpose is to illustrate the need to approach systemwide changes with care and caution, to understand the current system before making changes, to recognize significant differences among states' mental health systems, and to avoid a "one-size-fits-all" approach to system design. The perspective is that of the director of a psychiatric rehabilitation program who participated in the development of an effective psychiatric rehabilitation program, and later in her state's efforts to redesign the mental health and substance abuse systems.

Development of the Community Transition Program

The Community Transition Program (CTP) is a 40-bed psychiatric rehabilitation program within a 180-bed state hospital. The state hospital has three other programs, two of which have a statewide catchment (adolescent and family services and forensic services), and an acute program (short-term care) for adults that serves a sixteen-county area.

The CTP was inaugurated in 1982 after eight months of extensive planning with program staff and hospital administration, and collaboration with the psychology department of the local university. The CTP provided psychiatric rehabilitation to people with serious and persistent mental disorders who did not respond to short-term inpatient treatment (thirty to sixty days), who could not safely be treated in available community settings, and for whom no other program had been effective. The new program used key components of the social-learning condition of the large-scale outcome study of chronic inpatient treatment conducted by Gordon Paul (Paul and Lentz, 1977). The CTP began with a well-articulated mission statement and philosophy and a clear description of program design, staff role, and procedures for treatment planning and review. Additional rehabilitation modalities were incorporated, including the skill-training procedures developed at the University of California-Los Angeles Center for Rehabilitation of Schizophrenia, functional assessment and rehabilitation counseling approaches developed at Boston University, and cognitive and neuropsychological assessment and treatment (see Liberman, 1992).

As the CTP evolved, administrative obstacles emerged (Sullivan, Richardson, and Spaulding, 1991). The obstacles were in large part the traditional administrative and organizational structure of state hospitals. Changing those structures embodied some of the more sensitive issues in state hospital administration. The issues included the need for *program-level* management and accountability and the willingness to delegate program leadership to nonmedical professionals. The barriers were overcome largely by mandate from a key administrator, through new policy that carefully delineated administrative authority and distinguished between clinical and managerial prerogatives. The changes included a program administrative structure that was directly accountable for fulfillment of the program mission within budget, and implementation of the program design, including processes of admission, treatment planning and implementation, performance improvement, program development, staff hiring, and training. The role of the disciplinary departments or "services" changed, from direct supervision of individuals within the programs to supplying the programs with qualified staff and within-program clinical supervisors. The overall result was stronger authority within the administrative structure of each program, recognition of the clinical expertise and scope of practice of *all* professions within the programs, increased cost-effectiveness, and better outcome. By 1990, CTP had established effectiveness in returning people to the community. A formal program evaluation showed reductions in hospital use of 70 percent to 80 percent after treatment on the CTP, with an acceptable quality of life in aftercare environments (Sullivan, Richardson, and Spaulding, 1991).

By 1995, the CTP had established national and international visibility as a state-of-the-art, cost-effective psychiatric rehabilitation facility. The program mission and philosophy were clear. The staff were well trained, motivated, and busy with meaningful work, which translated into quality patient care. Hospitalwide surveys showed that the CTP staff performed especially well in understanding the purpose and philosophy of the program, their individual roles in the program, and the lines of clinical and administrative authority within the program. The hospital administration had gained a deep appreciation of the need for program-level management skills and structures, and for the values and technologies of psychiatric rehabilitation. A state hospital custodial back ward had been transformed into a clinically effective state-of-the-art rehabilitation program, at no additional cost to the state. The transition had included establishing and maintaining collaborative working relationships with community mental health center workers, as the hospital was not able to provide care after discharge. The fruits of the program's success were generally acknowledged to be the successful transition of the most treatment-resistant patients into residential programs, group homes, and apartments, with necessary mental health and substance abuse services and meaningful daily activities.

The Behavioral Health Redesign

Despite the CTP's successes, there were larger problems in the state mental health system. For years, there had been complaints that services were fragmented and that communities lacked the services needed to help people with serious and persistent mental disorders live in the community. The "Torrey report" (Torrey, Erdman, Wolfe, and Flynn, 1990) was highly critical of community-based services in the state. In various national surveys, the state had ranked in the lowest quartile in per capita mental health expenditures, and even worse in community-based services. By 1994, an accumulation of pressure from mental health professionals, consumers, and advocates had led the state legislature to undertake a number of studies and formal reviews of the mental health and substance abuse systems. One result was a legislative mandate to adopt the Medicaid Rehabilitation Option, a subsidy program that selectively supports community-based psychiatric rehabilitation and related activities. There had been historical political resistance to expanding the state's involvement in federal entitlement programs, and this had been one contributor to the insufficiency of community-based mental health services.

Momentum built for system reform. Spiraling Medicaid costs in both general health and mental health services contributed to a sense of urgency. Failure to resolve fiscal and policy disputes at the highest administrative levels led the governor to initiate administrative reorganization of the entire health and human services sector of the executive branch of government. The prospect of competition for shrinking resources activated rivalries among various divisions of the mental health provider community and intensified lobbying of legislative and executive branch officials. The legislature passed a law that mandated adoption of "managed care technology" in the public mental health system. The governor embraced this mandate. A private managed care company was contracted to administer Medicaid mental health services. A second managed care company was brought in as a "consultant" to that part of the bureaucracy whose administrative purview included the state hospitals. Additional private consultants were brought in to advise on reorganization of the mental health system.

One step ahead of these developments, the state mental health and substance abuse administration began a grassroots initiative to energize and guide reform, the Behavioral Health Redesign. This began with a series of professionally facilitated conferences and workshops, bringing together hundreds of stakeholders from across the state to evaluate the existing service systems and develop a "new vision" for public mental health services. The stakeholders included consumers, providers, administrators from all levels of the bureaucracy, and other interested parties. Special committees and task forces were created to follow up on the productions of the larger events. The Behavioral Health Redesign was overtaken by and incorporated into the broader reform activities across the health and human services system.

In keeping with the state's political tradition of grassroots populism, the reform process retained its inclusive participatory character. The various committees and task forces became deliberative bodies in which the administration's new policy proposals were evaluated. By the end of 1997, most of the high-level administrative reorganization had been completed, and the process focused increasingly on the particulars of mental health service organization, regulation, and delivery. However, at this point the process stalled. Administrators began to encounter the "devil in the details" of some key proposals. New services or new providers did not appear as expected. The governor's term ended in 1998. The new governor was of the opposing political party. Within a few months, none of the top administrators involved in the Behavioral Health Redesign were still in office, and its overall direction was being carefully reevaluated.

It is too early to conclude anything about the results of the activities of these six years, and a complete analysis would be beyond the scope of this discussion. The future remains obscure. However, as the process of deliberation and reform unfolded, much was revealed about future possibilities for state hospital–based psychiatric rehabilitation programs such as the CTP. The remainder of this case study focuses on those aspects of the process most pertinent to psychiatric rehabilitation and the roles of the state hospitals.

Perceptions of Rehabilitation and Managed Care

Early in the reform process, a view held by many was that too much of the state's mental health resources was tied up in its three state hospitals. A number of influential participants took the position that the state hospitals should be downsized. On the premise (among others) that there would be no new funding for public mental health services, it was argued that state hospital beds should be closed in order to generate money for "community programs." It was presumed that all current occupants of such beds could be served in intensive case management programs, backed up by emergency and short-term inpatient services. The legislative mandate for the Medicaid Rehabilitation Option was seen as a way to leverage more federal funds through subsidies for "community-based" services (Medicaid does not support institution-based services). High-level administrators began making public statements that state hospital beds occupied by recipients of rehabilitation would be closed and moved to community settings. Only forensic beds in the state hospitals would be exempt from a new wave of deinstitutionalization.

Outside the mental health community, the prospect of community-based care at lower cost than long-term state hospital–based care had considerable appeal. In addition, short-term hospitalization seemed to many to be something the private sector could provide, and privatization was generally a politically appealing concept.

As the argument to eliminate rehabilitation from the state hospitals proceeded, proposed policies and regulations to limit the availability of rehabilitation in community-based settings also began to appear. These took the form of "entry-and-exit criteria" (a managed care concept that identifies who is eligible for what services and when) and reimbursement rates for various services, including rehabilitation. Hospital-based services were dichotomized into "acute" and "secure," based on immediate levels of dangerousness, with no consideration of baseline levels of personal and social functioning. Eligibility criteria and funding levels for community-based rehabilitation were designed to reduce support services as soon as a patient is stabilized, with no attention to development of new adaptive skills or gradual improvement of functioning over time. Funding levels were clearly insufficient to provide rehabilitation over a time period necessary for a meaningful benefit to any but the *least* disabled recipients. It is arguable that the proposals reflected the clinical realities of private sector services for nondisabled recipients, but they were strikingly insensitive to the issues of severely and persistently ill, disabled patients in need of long-term rehabilitation. Ultimately, the proposals reflected a radically "medicalized" view of services, in which medication is the only known therapeutic agent, and people are incapable of change in response to psychosocial services, including rehabilitation. The proposals were recognizable recapitulations of policies and regulations used previously in other states in attempts to downsize the state hospitals, which had resulted in failure to accomplish any change except for cost shifts into the correctional system or precipitous increases in homelessness, mortality, and street crime. The work group responsible for deliberating the proposals regarding entry-and-exit criteria failed to reach consensus. The final product did not reflect an understanding of the needs of people with severe psychiatric disabilities, in either institutional or community settings.

Reaction and Course Correction

The emerging view of rehabilitation, which appeared to have the endorsement of influential figures in the state mental health administration, was subject to challenge on various grounds. The premise that all people with severe and disabling psychiatric disorders can be served in community settings and can be given sufficient support and emergency and inpatient services is not well supported in the research literature (see Monroe-DeVita and Mohatt, Chapter Seven). The premise that the public would not support increases in funding for mental health services was inconsistent with local survey data. The premise that any community setting, no matter how "secure," is inevitably cheaper than a setting of comparable security in a state hospital was not supported by actual cost figures, even with federal subsidies taken into account. Information was available on the experiences of other states where similar downsizing of state hospitals was unsuccessful. The premise of a meaningful difference between forensic patients and rehabilitation recipients was specious, as the administration found when it tried to discharge civilly committed patients. The question of why rehabilitation could not be provided to patients who remained in the state hospitals after the downsizing was never addressed.

However, what most blunted the drive to downsize was the skepticism of a number of state legislators, who came to doubt that the mental health administration could finesse a transfer of resources from the state hospitals to a community-based system yet to be constructed without any casualties. Their doubts were deepened by widespread complaints that although the reform process had the appearance of openness and inclusiveness, it was considerably less than that, serving mostly to create the illusion of public support for policies created by the administration in response to the advice of private consultants. "Community-based" providers, who had initially hoped to benefit from resources liberated by downsizing the state hospitals, became skeptical that the administration was really planning to return those resources to public mental health services at all. Providers, law enforcement administrators, consumers, advocates, and the public became alarmed by the prospect of underserved people in the streets, county jails, and prisons. Once again in response to the concerns of providers, consumers, and advocates, the legislature passed a law prohibiting downsizing before the availability of specific, appropriate community-based alternatives.

The slowing of the downsizing juggernaut created more opportunity for discussion and reappraisal of the premises behind it. For the CTP, this developed into four strategies. First, every opportunity was taken to educate key figures in the mental health administration about the cost-effectiveness of psychiatric rehabilitation, whether it is carried out in institutional or community settings. The cost-effectiveness argument was supported by a recent doctoral dissertation (Weilage, 1996) that had compared in detail the costs of the average course of rehabilitation in the CTP with the costs of supporting people in the community without the improved personal and social functioning that the CTP confers. Using fairly conservative assumptions about rehospitalization and the cost of community support for people not provided rehabilitation, the study found that rehabilitation in the CTP produces a cost *offset* within a few years after a patient's discharge.

The second strategy was to develop and disseminate a document, directed toward an audience of nonclinical administrators, that described the nature of psychiatric rehabilitation and its recipient population, with an emphasis on the established cost-effectiveness of the CTP. The document acknowledged the need for more and better community-based services for people with severe and disabling psychiatric disorders but also argued for a finely graduated system of institution- and community-based settings that would permit recipients to move gradually from higher- to lower-security environments. The document included a proposal to *expand* rather than *move* the CTP, so that rehabilitation could be provided all along the continuum of environments. This document was widely distributed to the state's planners, Behavioral Health Redesign authorities, providers, legislators, and consumer groups. It was referenced frequently in discussions with state authorities and planners.

The third strategy was to participate helpfully and seriously in as many venues as available in the Behavioral Health Redesign process. Because of the participatory process used by the state in planning the new behavioral health system, there were many opportunities available, beginning with the initial advisory group.

The fourth strategy was to continue to work together with community-based providers at the local level after the formal planning had been completed. An important benefit of the state's approach to creating a new behavioral system was bringing people together who had previously been working in isolation. People were brought together to work within a tight time frame on an important planning document that represented the behavioral health system they wanted in their region.

One particularly salient part of the CTP message was about the heterogeneity of the severely disabled psychiatric population. The CTP had always served the most treatment-resistant patients in the system. The program admission criteria codified this by requiring a *demonstrated failure to function adequately* in any available less restrictive setting. With a realistic view of the limitations of community-based programs, the natural clientele of the CTP can thus be more clearly identified. Also, restricting services to only the most severely disabled defines a very small subpopulation within the catchment, introducing consideration of economy of scale. In a state with large areas of low population density, it would be prohibitive to provide such high-intensity treatment to only a few patients at a time. Gradually, the "market niche" of the CTP became more apparent.

The proposal to expand the CTP into less restrictive environments found support on several fronts. It was generally consistent with the state's priority on developing new community-based services for state hospital residents. Collaborative planning with community providers in both the public and private sectors led to a joint project, a new twelve-bed residential program in the community, jointly staffed by state hospital, community mental health center, and private personnel, using CTP rehabilitation technology and serving patients whose functioning could take them one small step from institutional care. Thanks to a better understanding of the need for rehabilitation in the institution as well, the new unit was started without downsizing the original CTP.

Managed Care and the Future of Psychiatric Rehabilitation

So far, the roles of the state hospital and the CTP as providers of psychiatric rehabilitation have been preserved in the course of the Behavioral Health Redesign and related reform activities. In fact, the new community-based transitional program is setting new precedents, not only for the state hospital but also for state-local and public-private collaboration in mental health services. The next challenge will be to preserve psychiatric rehabilitation in a managed care environment. The process of translating visions and social policy into actual provision and regulation of mental health services has only just begun. The utilization review methods, the entry-and-exit criteria, the reimbursement rates, and related regulatory mechanisms in use now are those proposed when the Behavioral Health Redesign was dominated by a rush to downsize the state hospitals, by unrealistic beliefs about community-based care, and by misconceptions about psychiatric rehabilitation. They still reflect a disproportionate reliance on extraordinary social support and emergency and short-term inpatient treatment. They are insensitive to the value of producing baseline *improvements* in peoples' personal and social functioning. Recently, a CTP alumnus, now living with his family and unemployed, lost his eligibility for community support services, essentially because he can now ride his bicycle to appointments with his case manager.

On the one hand, this does not necessarily reflect a failure of managed care, which is simply a technology for implementing health care policy (see Searles and Fox, 1998). On the other hand, special care is needed to protect vulnerable individuals from hasty or insensitive applications of managed care (Hurley and Draper, 1998). If it is true that managed care practices reflect the social values and priorities of its client, then these regulatory mechanisms will gradually come to reflect public attitudes toward rehabilitation and quality of life. Ultimately, the outcome and cost-effectiveness research should convince a compassionate public that rehabilitation is worthwhile, wherever it takes place. However, we have already seen that social values can be overtaken by ill-informed and politicized bureaucracy, in its search for expedient solutions. It would be ironic, and tragic, if state hospitals were to survive in the twenty-first century, but psychiatric rehabilitation were to fall victim to simplistic nostrums myopically implemented to reduce mental health expenditures.

References

Hurley, R., and Draper, D. "Medicaid Managed Care for Special Needs Populations: Behavioral Health as 'Tracer Condition.'" In D. Mechanic (ed.), *Managed Behavioral Health Care: Current Realities and Future Potential.* New Directions for Mental Health Services, no. 78. San Francisco: Jossey-Bass, 1998.

Liberman, R. (ed.). *Handbook of Psychiatric Rehabilitation.* Old Tappan, N.J.: Macmillan, 1992.

Paul, G., and Lentz, R. *Psychosocial Treatment of Chronic Mental Patients: Milieu Versus Social-Learning Programs.* Cambridge, Mass.: Harvard University Press, 1977.

Searles, R., and Fox, R. "Behavioral Health: A View from the Industry." In D. Mechanic (ed.), *Managed Behavioral Health Care: Current Realities and Future Potential.* New Directions for Mental Health Services, no. 78. San Francisco: Jossey-Bass, 1998.

Sullivan, M., Richardson, C., and Spaulding, W. "University-State Hospital Collaboration in an Inpatient Psychiatric Rehabilitation Program." *Community Mental Health Journal,* 1991, *27* (6), 441–453.

Torrey, E., Erdman, K., Wolfe, S., and Flynn, L. *Care of the Seriously Mentally Ill: A Rating of State Programs.* (3rd ed.) Washington, D.C.: Public Citizen Health Research Group and the National Alliance for the Mentally Ill, 1990.

Weilage, M. "Outcome and Cost-Effectiveness in a Psychiatric Rehabilitation Program." Unpublished doctoral dissertation, Department of Psychology, University of Nebraska-Lincoln, 1996.

MARY SULLIVAN is program director of the Community Transition Program, Lincoln Regional Center, and adjunct assistant professor in the Department of Psychology at the University of Nebraska-Lincoln.

Part Two

The Role of New Technologies

Current trends in forensic mental health services and how they are used are shaping the future of state hospitals and mental health systems.

No Place Else to Go: The Changing Role of State Hospitals and Forensic Mental Health Services

Mario J. Scalora

This chapter is a discussion of the various factors that are shaping the nature of state hospital–based forensic mental health services and that are therefore expected to shape the future role of the state hospitals themselves.

Shifts in Forensic Services and Populations

The very meaning of "forensic mental health services" is shifting. Traditionally, forensic services are assessments of persons with serious mental illnesses who are facing adjudication. The purpose of the assessment is to determine competency to stand trial or to advise the court about the person's mental state at the time of the offense. More recently, forensic assessment is increasingly seen as helpful in advising the court about the disposition of people who have already been adjudicated. This might include advice about the sentence or the type of treatment most appropriate for someone found to be not guilty or not responsible for a crime by reason of insanity. Most recently, forensic resources are increasingly utilized in civil contexts, for example, with civilly committed persons who are "unmanageable" within other sectors of care, or convicted sex offenders who have been indefinitely committed under sexual predator statutes.

This trend reflects, in part, a growing reliance by the courts on the specialized knowledge and assessment technology of forensic psychology. Although the empirical database on the various behavioral phenomena associated with "criminal," "socially unacceptable," and "dangerous" behavior remains quite limited, available knowledge and technology does allow some reduction of uncertainty, in ways that enhance the courts' decision making (Steadman, Rosenstein, MacAskill, and Manderscheid, 1988).

It is also the case that forensic considerations are playing a bigger role in the design and administration of mental health services, especially in the public sector. One factor behind this trend is a heightened public perception of mental illness as being strongly related to violence (Steadman and others, 1998). People with mental illness have always been stigmatized as being more violent than they really are, but sensationalistic media coverage has made this worse over the past few years. In addition, one effect of deinstitutionalization and community-based treatment is that the few truly dangerous people in the traditional state hospital population are more likely to have opportunity to engage in violent behavior. In reality, mental patients involved with the legal system are a heterogeneous group with regard to risk of violence to the community (Steadman and others, 1998). Though this requires a highly individualized approach to clinical decision making, facilities and systems must have the capability of timely and appropriate administrative response to case-by-case judgments. Further, as public and private mental health services are increasingly penetrated by cost management structures, risk for violent behavior becomes a significant consideration in the development of policy on service utilization, cost containment, and systemic restructuring (Borum, 1996). *Risk assessment* has become one of the most important items in the forensic clinician's tool box. The management of risk is becoming a preoccupation of mental health clinicians and administrators.

The shifts in forensic services and the infusion of forensic considerations into mental health policy and system design can be seen in several relatively separate domains, all of which are pertinent to the future role of state hospitals. For the purposes of this discussion, these domains include criminalization of people with mental illness, cost containment and system reform, and inclusion of new forensic subpopulations.

Criminalization of the Mentally Ill

There is growing suspicion that one of the consequences of mental health system "reform" is a shift of costs and people into the correctional system. This shift has been called the "criminalization of the mentally ill" (Briar, 1983; Torrey and others, 1992). Similarly, some commentators have suggested that deinstitutionalization from state hospitals has resulted in *reinstitutionalization* into jails and prisons (Emery, Glover, and Mazade, 1998). Although there is little published research to verify this suspicion directly and conclusively, media reports, state agency statistics, and indirectly related research findings provide cause for concern.

There has been a steady trend toward larger jail and prison populations, associated with tougher sentencing policies, across the country (Gilliard and Beck, 1998). A substantial proportion of these inmates are in need of mental health treatment (Beers, 1996). In addition to detaining individuals pending arraignment and holding them awaiting trial, adjudication, or sentencing, jails in some jurisdictions hold noncriminally accused persons with mental illness pending their movement to appropriate treatment facilities (Gilliard and Beck, 1998). The impact of increased numbers of persons with mental illness in jails led one commentator to refer to jails as "enduring asylums" (Briar, 1983, p. 388).

The percentage of jail detainees with mental disorders is substantially higher than that of the general population (Steadman and Veysey, 1997; Teplin, 1984). Powell, Holt, and Fondacaro (1997) reviewed empirical studies determining rates of mental illness within urban jails and reported that the patterns in urban jail and prison studies indicated "a clear pattern of rates of serious mental illness that far exceeded those found in the general population" (p. 429). Press reports (Hornbeck, 1997) assert that the number of prison inmates in Michigan who were former patients in state mental hospitals has ballooned by 23 percent over the past four years, more than double the 11 percent increase in the state's overall prison population. This is occurring as the state has been downsizing its state psychiatric hospitals. Jails across the nation are accommodating an estimated 640,000 to 800,000 detainees with mental disabilities annually (Rubin and McCampbell, 1995). Approximately 17 percent of male and 25 percent of female detainees had taken medication prescribed for mental or emotional difficulties prior to being jailed, and 10 percent of males and 15 percent of females had prior admissions to mental health facilities (Harlow, 1998).

Jails are generally poorly equipped to provide treatment for persons with mental illness, despite being increasingly viewed as alternatives to inadequate community-based mental health services (Teplin and Pruett, 1995; Torrey and others, 1992). A recent national survey (Steadman and Veysey, 1997) indicated that at most, 10 percent of jail detainees receive mental health services. These services are typically very limited, only rarely including suicide risk-screening, medication, evaluation, special housing, or psychosocial programming. Further, persons with mental illnesses who come into contact with the criminal justice system present a proportionally higher level of special needs warranting particular attention (for example, recurring substance use disorders, homelessness, HIV-AIDS).

In a state that has been prominent in downsizing its state hospitals, the U.S. Department of Justice is threatening Los Angeles County with a federal lawsuit if "deliberate indifference" to the medical needs of inmates with mental illness is not corrected (Daunt, 1997, p. B4). The California correctional system was cited by the U.S. District Court as having shown deliberate indifference to the needs of mentally disordered inmates. The court called for the appointment of a special master to improve the correctional system's care of the 11 to 15 percent of the inmates with mental disorders ("Judge Critical of Prisoners' Treatment," 1995).

If in fact there has been a shift in funding and people from the mental health system to the correctional system, there are probably many reasons for it. These could include lingering public (and legislative) stigmatization and ignorance about mental illness, the differential willingness of legislatures to appropriate funds for correctional instead of mental health services, ill-informed judicial practices, and cynical mental health bureaucracies that promote simplistic low-cost service models and fail to advocate for patient needs. An optimistic hypothesis is that this is a time-limited phenomenon, the temporary result of unrealistic hopes that new treatment and case management approaches would permit downsizing of state hospitals without such consequences. However, this is reminiscent of the false hopes and transinstitutionalization of previous decades (see Bachrach, Chapter One, and discussion in Chapter Two). The previous experience did not prevent the present one, and the optimistic hypothesis may be as naive as the false expectations themselves.

It seems more likely that a true solution to the problem will have to be a comprehensive reconceptualization of the nature of forensic mental health services and their appropriate venues. Perhaps some members of the ballooning mentally ill prison population should be returned to state hospitals. Others may be more appropriately served in nontraditional correctional services that would include psychiatric case management, enhanced discharge planning, diversion services, forensic clinics, and community support programs (McDonald and Teitelbaum, 1994; Steadman and Veysey, 1997). However, such a diversified system would require astute judgments about which services are needed by which individuals. Clinical and psychopathological considerations will ultimately have to complement social values and legal concepts of guilt and culpability. This is another point at which forensic clinical services must work hand in hand with a forensic perspective on system administration.

Cost Containment and System Reform

Cost containment is one of the principal realities of health care policy today. In the public mental health sector, cost containment activities generally include outright downsizing and defunding of existing facilities and services; adoption of managed care "technology"; emulation in the public sector of private sector management practices; privatization of clinical and administrative services; and reorganization of state, county, and municipal agencies and their relationships.

State hospitals have been a primary target for changes related to cost containment. More state psychiatric facilities were closed during the 1990s than during the previous two decades combined. Almost half of the country's existing state psychiatric facilities are facing either downsizing or reorganization (Emery, Glover, and Mazade, 1998). Redick, Witkin, Atay, and Manderscheid (1994) reported that as a result of downsizing activity, inpatient populations within state psychiatric facilities decreased by 77 percent between 1970 and 1992. These changes are sometimes directly associated with system reorganization (Lutterman, 1994; see McDonel, Meyer, and Deliberty, 1996 for a specific state example). Privatization of state hospital functions is also increasing, as seventeen states are now outsourcing the operation and management of at least sixty-six hospitals (National Association of State Mental Health Program Directors, 1997).

State hospitals are the historical site for forensic mental health services. There is a substantial fiscal incentive for using cost containment practices for forensic services, as state revenues are the primary source (Beers, 1996). Nevertheless, the general trends of cost containment and system reform have moved more slowly in forensic venues. There are rational reasons for this. Management models derived from private sector services make false assumptions about the primary object of management, the recipients' *treatment-seeking behavior.* In forensic populations, and increasingly in the public mental health sector at large, treatment-seeking behavior is not often initiated by the recipient, but by others affected by the person's disruptive behavior (Cuffel, 1997). The highest-cost users in a mental health system are less likely to perceive their behavior as problematic for themselves, less likely to adhere to treatment regimens, and more likely to be involved within the criminal justice system (Cuffel, 1997). Thus, these are exactly the recipients to whom a managed care process would tend to deny access to services. Failure to do so puts the managed care entity at significant financial risk, especially in a capitated system.

Similarly, services cannot be withheld (or not reimbursed) from these individuals at the managed care entity's discretion. To a significant extent, it remains the prerogative of judicial or civil commitment authorities to determine "level of care," that is, where the recipient is to be served. The profitability of a managed care system usually depends on providing the "lowest" (that is, cheapest) level of care possible. This usually means minimizing use of hospital- or institution-based services.

The rational strategy for a managed care entity is to avoid fiscal responsibility for forensic service recipients, or any involuntary recipients for that matter. Those individuals must be served, however, so forensic services are "carved out" of the managed care contract so that potentially costly recipients can be served there as involuntary or forensic patients. This could be one cause of *cost shifting* secondary to cost containment activity. The costs of serving individuals in the parts of the system contracted to managed care are shifted to other parts, that is, forensic services. Over time, this could also be one source of the overall increase in the forensic population (Beers, 1996), projected to grow by 25 percent between now and 2010 (Goldsmith, Manderscheid, Sacks, and Henderson, 1994). Underserved patients tend to become "forensic" or at least involuntary recipients as their functioning deteriorates and they eventually encounter legal problems or become dangerous. Thus, a "forensic carve-out" may contain costs from a managed care entity's perspective, but it is not necessarily in the public interest or the interests of the patients. In the end, it may actually increase the cost to the public of serving the population, whether in a forensic or nonforensic setting.

There are other, equally rational, and perhaps more legitimate, reasons for limiting use of private sector managed care practices with forensic populations

(Packer, 1998). These include problems associated with the characteristics of severe and persistent mental illness in general (Durham, 1994; Reed, 1994), as well as mentally ill forensic patients in particular. Clinicians who treat forensic patients require special expertise to ensure that assessment, treatment, and disposition are consistent with the patients' legal circumstances. Forensic clinicians also require special expertise in assessment and management of risk and in clinical management of violent behavior. Even with competent staff, mistakes are inevitably made, sometimes with disastrous and highly publicized consequences. Even when there are no mistakes, the risk levels in the population are such that tragedies must be expected and managed when they occur (Reichlin and Bloom, 1993). This raises questions about the liabilities and accountabilities that can be reasonably expected with private managed care administration. Finally, state mental health services usually enjoy some degree of sovereign immunity from civil actions related to clinical decisions, and it is very unclear how much this could be extended to private contractors. Liability could significantly increase the cost of providing services to forensic populations.

As an alternative to formal utilization of managed care technology, some states have attempted to cut costs by decentralizing forensic evaluation activity. Although institutions still maintain a significant role in forensic evaluation and treatment, a majority of states rely primarily on less costly outpatient evaluations performed primarily by community-based providers with regional or local catchment areas (Grisso and others, 1996). However, a substantial majority of states still utilize forensic hospitals with statewide catchment areas to provide services to complement community-based services (Grisso and others, 1996).

The major impact of cost containment and system reform activities on forensic mental health services has been indirect, a result of those activities on other parts of the system. The most common impact is increased pressure on forensic services, resulting from elimination of nonforensic state hospital resources and from legislative and judicial mandates to provide services to various subpopulations. With the reductions of beds traditionally available to civilly committed patients, a significant number of remaining state-funded psychiatric beds are becoming earmarked for forensic patients. For example, people found not guilty of a crime by reason of insanity now occupy half of the long-term public psychiatric beds in the state of Missouri, compared to 9 percent in 1981 (Linhorst and Dirks-Linhorst, 1997). Few of these patients are initially placed in community-based facilities. This pattern indicates a disproportionate shift of resources.

Forensic facilities increasingly receive displaced individuals with severe and persistent mental illness for court-ordered evaluation and treatment related to criminal processing issues (for example, competency to stand trial and responsibility at the time of offense), as well as inmates transferred from jails and prisons for inpatient psychiatric care. Jail administrators are facing increased legal liability pressure to transfer detainees with mental illness to more appropriate treatment (Rubin and McCampbell, 1995). Another significant subgroup of forensic admissions includes civilly committed patients deemed unmanageable in other hospital settings (Beers, 1996).

In addition to the pressure resulting from an increased number of admissions, forensic providers also face difficulty discharging patients into community-based levels of care from inpatient and secure settings (Beers, 1996). The intensity of the referral issues triggering entry into forensic facilities through either civil or criminal routes, as well as the violent histories of forensic patients, makes discharge planning difficult. Community providers are often reticent and ill equipped to accept responsibility for multineed patients discharged from forensic facilities. Given community concerns about safety, forensic facilities are faced with significant pressure to manage their flow of patients. The management of patient flow is further complicated by the limited number of aftercare or conditional-release options available for those persons with serious forensic legal designations such as not guilty by reason of insanity (Bloom, Williams, and Bigelow, 1991; Heilbrun and Griffin, 1993).

Complicating risk assessment issues even further is the fact that such patients tend to have a different clinical presentation than nonforensic patients, as they are more likely to be viewed as higher functioning and have higher prevalence of personality disorder and substance abuse diagnoses (Linhorst and Dirks-Linhorst, 1997). Even if primary symptom management issues related to mental illness are successfully addressed in treatment, clinicians also must contend with the significantly higher risk of reoffense secondary to characterological issues such as psychopathy (Serin, 1996). Administrators and clinicians must also reconcile the potential competition for limited state resources between forensic and nonforensic clientele within facilities as well as milieu management issues that may occur with the mixing of forensic and nonforensic patients.

In summary, cost containment and system reform have intensified and complicated the role of forensic services in state hospitals. There has been some experimentation with decentralization and deinstitutionalization of forensic services, but the impact has been minor compared with the increase in pressure on state hospital–based services. As with the issue of criminalization of the mentally ill, there is cause for concern that some aspects of cost containment and reform are actually creating cost *shifting* and a *larger* population in need of forensic services.

Inclusion of New Forensic Subpopulations

Recent legislative developments increasingly require state hospitals to serve patients who do not meet the diagnostic criteria of severe and persistent mental illness but who present primarily with impulsive or characterological disorders. This is particularly true of laws dealing with sex offenders.

A generation of "sexual psychopath" and "sexual predator" statutes in numerous states provide for civil commitment of prisoners who, after serving their sentence, remain at high risk to reoffend. Such statutes appear to be a de facto broadening of the definition of mental disorder, and therefore of commitment criteria, to include a *predisposition* to sexually act out (see Grubin, 1997; Schopp, Scalora, and Pearce, in press). The statutes were recently upheld by the U.S. Supreme Court in *Kansas* v. *Hendricks* (1997). The Court in *Hendricks* required the state to establish that the subject of the commitment hearing suffers from either a "mental abnormality" or a "personality disorder" and that this disorder renders the person likely to commit sexual offenses. This virtually assures that the locus of continued incarceration will be forensic units in state hospitals. Even prior to the reaffirmation of this practice by the Supreme Court, sex offenders were the prevalent category of patients housed in forensic facilities who are charged with a crime (Beers, 1996).

The cost of implementing sexual predator statutes is substantial (La Fond, 1998). A survey of state mental health agencies indicates that the annual cost of providing inpatient services in state mental health agency forensic units ranges from $60,000 to more than $125,000 per person, compared with $25,000 to $35,000 per person for inpatient services in state corrections facilities. The administrative and litigation costs inherent in the implementation of such statutes are significant components. The potentially extensive length of stay of committed sex offenders threatens to compound the aforementioned patient flow problems of forensic services.

Forensic mental health services are generally predisposed to providing *offense-specific* treatment and risk assessment. This approach is different from the symptom or *disorder-specific* treatment approaches necessary for persons with serious thought or emotional disorder. Expanding mandates to provide offense-specific treatment inevitably diverts resources from treatment of other state hospital recipients, even within forensic services. Increased civil commitment to state hospitals of high-risk sex offenders could alter the entire mission of state mental health agencies and drain resources from services for persons with diagnosable mental illness (National Association of State Mental Health Program Directors, 1997).

Conclusions

Pressures for cost containment and reform in the broader mental health service delivery system have resulted in increased numbers of persons with serious mental illness requiring forensic mental health services. Increasing numbers of persons with serious mental illness are found in correctional settings ill equipped to serve this population. People with serious and disabling mental illness in state hospitals must increasingly compete for resources with (often treatment-refractory) sexual offenders committed as a result of sexual predator statutes. Criminalization of the mentally ill is complemented by the "medicalization of criminals." The irony is compounded by the fact that these circumstances have been created by social policy that seeks to reduce the costs of psychiatric care without due regard to safety, interacting with social policy that seeks safety at any cost.

If these trends continue, the future role of state hospitals will clearly be forensic, but not psychiatric. The public's desire for safety must be respected, but this does not require acquiescence to ill-considered but temporarily expedient solutions. The public interest is best served by a balanced consideration of safety, compassion, and *long-term cost-effectiveness*. It is *not* cost-effective to treat people with impulse control and personality disorders in settings designed for the treatment of severe and disabling mental illness. The outcome research indicates that it *is* cost-effective to provide treatment and rehabilitation, rather than cheaper custodial care, to even the most severely disabled mentally ill people in forensic state hospital settings (see Stuve and Menditto, Chapter Three).

The situation seems to demand some fundamental reconceptualization about forensic services, populations, and venues. There are a number of distinct populations who benefit from forensic mental health services. Some of these populations are the historical recipients of state hospital–based services, others are historically prison inmates, and still others have no clear history. Where people are served is best determined by systematic analysis of specific needs and resources, not by the unintended vicissitudes of social policy and ad hoc reactions to court decisions. Though all these populations have a need for "forensic" services, they also have specific and unique needs that must be taken into account. At the same time, competent forensic mental health services require specially and broadly trained professionals, familiar with the characteristics of all these populations and the settings that serve them.

A more hopeful vision of the future state hospital includes a prominence of forensic services, but tailored to the needs of specific populations explicitly included in the hospital's service mission. It seems highly likely that a small but significant group of people with severe and disabling mental illness will need psychiatric rehabilitation in state hospitals or comparable settings because of their forensic status. For these recipients, rehabilitation must be complemented by the psycholegal and risk management services that are the familiar domain of forensic professionals. Forensic professionals will have to collaborate with rehabilitation professionals and administrators to make this happen. Future analyses may conclude that other populations could be cost effectively served in state hospital settings, especially if those settings are adapted to the purpose. If so, it will be important to ensure that forensic services and treatment services remain complementary and that other populations are not displaced to less appropriate settings.

Finally, it seems clear that the future role of forensic services, in state hospitals and elsewhere, must be worked out with a perspective on the entire health and human services system. State hospitals will not be the insular institutions they have been in the past. Service recipients will move across settings as their needs change. Similarly, providers of forensic services must be prepared to distribute their activities across the entire system. Ultimately, this means that forensic mental health professionals must involve themselves in social policy development and service-planning processes.

References

Beers, J. *Survey of State Security Mental Health Facilities Results.* Unpublished manuscript, 1996.

Bloom, J., Williams, M., and Bigelow, D. "Monitored Conditional Release of Persons Found Not Guilty by Reason of Insanity." *American Journal of Psychiatry,* 1991, *148,* 444–448.

Borum, R. "Improving the Clinical Practice of Violence Risk Assessment: Technology, Guidelines, and Training." *American Psychologist,* 1996, *51,* 945–956.

Briar, K. H. "Jails: Neglected Asylums." *Social Casework,* 1983, *64,* 387–393.

Cuffel, B. "Disruptive Behavior and the Determinants of Costs in the Public Mental Health System." *Psychiatric Services,* 1997, *48,* 1562–1566.

Daunt, T. "Jails Must Alter Care of Mentally Ill." *Los Angeles Times,* Sept. 6, 1997, p. B4.

Durham, M. "Healthcare's Greatest Challenge: Providing Services to People with Severe Mental Illness in Managed Care." *Behavioral Science and the Law,* 1994, *12,* 331–349.

Emery, B., Glover, R., and Mazade, N. "The Environmental Trends Facing State Mental Health Agencies." *Administration and Policy in Mental Health,* 1998, *25,* 337–347.

Gilliard, D., and Beck, A. *Prison and Jail Inmates at Midyear 1997.* (National Criminal Justice Reference Service publication no. 167247.) Washington, D. C.: U.S. Department of Justice, 1998.

Goldsmith, H., Manderscheid, R., Sacks, A., and Henderson, M. "Inpatient Admissions to Specialty Mental Health Organizations: Forecasts 1990 to 2010." *Administration and Policy in Mental Health,* 1994, *22,* 71–84.

Grisso, T., and others. "A National Survey of Hospital- and Community-Based Approaches to Pretrial Mental Health Evaluations." *Psychiatric Services,* 1996, *47,* 642–644.

Grubin, D. "Inferring Predictors of Risk: Sex Offenders." *International Review of Psychiatry,* 1997, *9,* 225–231.

Harlow, C. *Profile of Jail Inmates, 1996.* (National Criminal Justice Reference Service publication no. 164620.) Washington, D. C.: U.S. Department of Justice, 1998.

Heilbrun, K., and Griffin, P. "Community-Based Treatment of Insanity Acquittees." *International Journal of Law and Psychiatry,* 1993, *16,* 133–150.

Hornbeck, M. "Mentally Ill Flood Michigan's Prisons." *Detroit News,* Dec. 4, 1997, p. A1.

"Judge Critical of Prisoners' Treatment." *Associated Press,* Sept. 14, 1995.

Kansas v. *Hendricks,* 117 S.Ct. 2072 (1997).

La Fond, J. Q. "The Costs of Enacting a Sexual Predator Law." *Psychology, Public Policy, and Law,* 1998, *4,* 468–504.

Linhorst, D., and Dirks-Linhorst, P. "The Impact of Insanity Acquittees on Missouri's Public Mental Health System." *Law and Human Behavior,* 1997, *21,* 327–338.

Lutterman, T. "The State Mental Health Agency Profile System." In R. Manderscheid and M. Sonnenschein (eds.), *Mental Health, United States, 1994.* Center for Mental Health Services. (Department of Health and Human Services publication no. SMA 94-3000.) Washington, D.C.: U.S. Government Printing Office, 1994.

McDonald, D., and Teitelbaum, M. "Managing Mentally Ill Offenders in the Community: Milwaukee's Community Support Program." (National Criminal Justice Reference Service publication no. 145330.) Washington, D.C.: U.S. Department of Justice, 1994.

McDonel, E., Meyer, L., and Deliberty, R. "Implementing State-Level Mental Health Policy Reforms in Indiana: Closing a State-Operated Psychiatric Hospital and Passing Major Mental Health Reform Legislation." *International Journal of Law and Psychiatry,* 1996, *19,* 239–264.

National Association of State Mental Health Program Directors. *Closing and Reorganizing State Psychiatric Hospitals: 1996.* State Mental Health Agency Profile System Highlights. Alexandria, Va.: National Association of State Mental Health Program Directors, Dec. 1997.

Packer, I. "Privatized Managed Care and Forensic Mental Health Services." *Journal of the American Academy of Psychiatry and the Law,* 1998, *26,* 123–129.

Powell, T., Holt., J., and Fondacaro, K. "The Prevalence of Mental Illness Among Inmates in a Rural State." *Law and Human Behavior,* 1997, *21,* 427–438.

Redick, R., Witkin, M., Atay, J., and Manderscheid, R. *The Evolution and Expansion of Mental Health Care in the United States Between 1955 and 1990.* Mental Health Statistical Note, no. 210. Rockville, Md.: Substance Abuse and Mental Health Services Administration, 1994.

Reed, S. "Serious Mental Illness and Capitation Financing." *Behavioral Science and the Law,* 1994, *12,* 379–388.

Reichlin, S., and Bloom, J. "Effects of Publicity on a Forensic Hospital." *Bulletin of the American Academy of Psychiatry and the Law,* 1993, *21,* 475–483.

Rubin, P., and McCampbell, S. "The Americans with Disabilities Act and Criminal Justice: Providing Inmate Services." *National Institute of Justice Research in Action.* (National Criminal Justice Reference Service publication no. 148139.) Washington, D.C.: U.S. Department of Justice, 1995.

Schopp, R., Scalora, M., and Pearce, M. "Expert Testimony and Professional Judgment: Psychological Expertise and Commitment as a Sexual Predator After *Hendricks.*" *Psychology, Public Policy, and Law,* in press.

Serin, R. "Violent Recidivism in Criminal Psychopaths." *Law and Human Behavior,* 1996, *20,* 207–217.

Steadman, H. J., Rosenstein, M. J., MacAskill, R. L., and Manderscheid, R. W. "A Profile of Mentally Disordered Offenders Admitted to Inpatient Psychiatric Services in the United States." *Law and Human Behavior,* 1988, *12,* 91–99.

Steadman, H., and Veysey, B. "Providing Services for Jail Inmates with Mental Disorders." *National Institute of Justice Research in Brief.* (National Criminal Justice Reference Service publication no. 162207.) Washington, D.C.: U.S. Department of Justice, 1997.

Steadman, H. J., and others. "Violence by People Discharged from Acute Psychiatric Inpatient Facilities and by Others in the Same Neighborhoods." *Archives of General Psychiatry,* 1998, *55,* 393–401.

Teplin, L. "Criminalizing Mental Disorder: The Comparative Arrest Rate of the Mentally Ill." *American Psychologist,* 1984, *39,* 794–803.

Teplin, L., and Pruett, N. "Police as Streetcorner Psychiatrists: Managing the Mentally Ill." *International Journal of Law and Psychiatry,* 1995, *15,* 139–156.

Torrey, E., and others. *Criminalizing the Seriously Mentally Ill: The Abuse of Jails as Mental Hospitals.* Washington, D.C.: Public Citizen Health Research Group and the National Alliance for the Mentally Ill, 1992.

MARIO J. SCALORA is assistant professor in the Department of Psychology in the Clinical Psychology Training Program and Law-Psychology Program at the University of Nebraska-Lincoln and a consulting clinical psychologist in the Forensic Mental Health Services, Lincoln Regional Center.

If the law provided for accessible and efficient means to facilitate mental health treatment, the law itself could be a component of the comprehensive care system.

The Psychiatric Hospital and Therapeutic Jurisprudence: Applying the Law to Promote Mental Health

Eric B. Elbogen, Alan J. Tomkins

Consider the following hypothetical psychiatric hospital discharge scenarios:

Phil is a fifty-eight-year-old male dually diagnosed with paranoid schizophrenia and alcohol abuse, hospitalized for one and a half months on an acute psychiatric unit because of increased psychosis and heavy drinking. After becoming stabilized on psychotropic medications, he was discharged back to his own apartment, with aftercare plans to take his medications daily, to see a psychiatrist once every month, and to attend Alcoholics Anonymous meetings five times a week. Within ten days of discharge, Phil became inebriated, attempted to choke one of his neighbors to death, and was subsequently arrested and rehospitalized.

Ellen is a thirty-two-year-old female diagnosed with bipolar disorder who was discharged to a residential program after a ten-month stay in the state psychiatric hospital. Three days after discharge, Ellen asked her case manager if her civil commitment had ended. Her case manager answered that Ellen's civil commitment had, indeed, ended once she was released from the hospital. The next day, Ellen did not show up at day treatment, left her residential program without telling staff or taking her medications, and was found seven weeks later in a neighboring state wandering the streets without food or shelter, floridly psychotic. The authorities in the neighboring state placed her into one of their psychiatric facilities.

Although there might be instances in which a patient's relapse in the community is beyond an inpatient clinician's foresight, there are many other instances in which the risk for failure is known to, or is at least knowable by, the clinician. Often, however, the clinician (or, more broadly, the psychiatric hospital) is hamstrung because of specific restrictions in legal rules and policies or a lack of legal options. What if, after discharge, there were legal provisions allowing the clinician (or hospital) to rely on the same kinds of contingencies that allowed a patient to progress to the point of discharge? What if legal rules and policies, instead of erecting a complex, bureaucratic process that severs the clinician's link to the discharged patient, were to make it easy for the clinician to follow up with necessary mental health treatments? What if the law allowed the clinician to maintain a legally sanctioned, therapeutic connection to a patient even after the patient's discharge from a psychiatric hospital? Such provisions seem almost unimaginable in a sociolegal context in which "bright lines" are drawn between the criteria required to involuntarily institutionalize someone and the conditions that require release from the hospital.

Many clinicians have found the law and its rules to be contrary to the mental health needs of patients. Legal criteria for civil commitment define clinical populations in psychiatric hospitals but often do not include explicit reference to a patient's treatment needs. Some legal commentators, however, are suggesting that there can be a much closer alliance between the mental health system and the justice system. An innovative conceptual framework called Therapeutic Jurisprudence(TJ) has emerged in the last decade, with the explicit goal of closing the schism between mental health objectives and justice objectives (see Sales, 1995; Symposium, 1992, 1993; Tomkins and Carson, in press; Wexler, 1991a; Wexler and Winick, 1991, 1996; Winick, 1997). At its core, TJ is a theoretical perspective from which to view mental health law as a source of patients' rights as well as a source for promoting (or thwarting) patients' mental health needs (Wexler, 1992). Acknowledging the centrality of patient rights in mental health law, TJ encourages not stopping there. TJ urges investigation into how the law can advance not just the rights of patients but also their beneficial therapeutic outcomes (Wexler and Schopp, 1992). TJ asks us to reframe how we understand mental health law by searching for ways to encourage both a patient's autonomy *and* psychological well-being. TJ prompts us to examine aspects of a patient's interactions with the law that can lead to useful clinical interventions.

Wexler (1998, p. 320) draws our attention to what he calls "psycholegal soft spots." Psycholegal soft spots represent vulnerabilities that frustrate a person's well-being but at the same time represent opportunities, resulting from the patient's legal situation, to promote mental health. A patient being discharged from the psychiatric hospital illustrates this concept. Patients released from involuntary hospitalization undergo a change in legal status, regaining a number of rights and liberties they had previous to civil commitment. When viewed from a TJ perspective, this change in legal status also has potential therapeutic implications and generates important questions central to treatment in psychiatric hospitals. Do discharged patients have the coping skills to adapt to their environment with this change in legal status? Does this transformation occur so rapidly and drastically as to undermine the patient's psychological well-being and former treatment gains? If so, what legal mechanisms can be used to lessen the impact of this change? With respect to the scenarios presented above, could Phil have benefited from a discharge plan that had more legal backing, such as an involuntary outpatient commitment? Might Ellen have been more compliant with aftercare plans if she had been transitioned more slowly into the community? If the law provided for accessible and efficient means to facilitate mental health treatment, the law itself could be a component of the comprehensive care system.

Therapeutic Jurisprudence: Injecting Mental Health into Legal Analysis

For the most part, mental health law and policy have been influenced by a *doctrinal analysis paradigm* of legal interests, characterized by "rights talk" (Keilitz, 1992, p. 2, citing Glendon, 1991). In other words, in the wake of legal reforms that culminated in the 1970s and specifically afforded basic legal protections to involuntary psychiatric patients, the psycholegal analysis of patients' issues has focused on patients' rights (see Perlin, 1989). Rights examinations—to the virtual exclusion of other concerns—too often have led to "sterile" and irrelevant mental health law, policy, and research (see, for example, Shah, 1978; Wexler, 1991b, 1993). Under narrow rights approaches, too often the law, policy, and research have ignored the therapeutic goals of patients and providers. The guiding orientation of TJ is to examine mental health and justice systems' interactions to ascertain "the extent to which substantive rules, legal procedures, and the roles of lawyers and judges produce therapeutic or antitherapeutic consequences" (Wexler and Winick, 1991, p. ix). In order to discern whether therapeutic outcomes are occurring, or if not then why not, TJ focuses on the relationships and interactions between the justice system and the mental health system.

TJ views the law itself as a potential "therapeutic agent" (Wexler, 1995, p. 220; Wexler, 1991b, p. 8; see also Wexler, 1991a, 1992; Wexler and Schopp, 1992; Wexler and Winick, 1991). The purpose of TJ scholarship, writes Professor David Wexler, is to "identify—and ultimately to examine empirically—relationships between legal arrangements and therapeutic outcomes. The research task is a cooperative and thoroughly interdisciplinary one (potentially involving law, philosophy, psychiatry, psychology, social work, criminal justice, public health and other fields). Such research should then usefully inform policy determinations regarding law reform" (Wexler, 1991b, p. 8).

TJ seeks developments in legal rules, practices, and roles that will promote effective mental health (that is, therapeutic) services without compromising other important values in mental health law and policy. It potentially helps fill the void that exists regarding useful, empirical research on issues concerning mental health law and policy.

In the last several years, there has been a significant amount of research and scholarship either inspired by TJ or consistent with its orientation (see, for example, Slobogin, 1995; Wexler, 1990, 1995; Wexler and Winick, 1991, 1996; Winick, 1997). Much of the work has integrated legal analysis with already existing psychological data or theory in order to suggest legal modifications that would produce therapeutic, rather than counter-therapeutic, effects of law (Slobogin, 1995; Wexler, 1995). Specifically, the initial work in TJ has been characterized by "four overlapping areas of inquiry: (a) the role of the law in producing psychological dysfunction, (b) therapeutic aspects of legal rules, (c) therapeutic aspects of legal procedures, and (d) therapeutic aspects of judicial and legal roles" (Wexler and Schopp, 1992, p. 362; see also Wexler, 1991a). The TJ framework fills a need in the mental health–justice systems area by contributing to the reconceptualization of mental health law and policy (see Petrila, 1995). As Slobogin concludes, TJ, "carefully pursued, will help produce a critical psychology that will force policymakers to pay more attention to the actual, rather than assumed, impact of the law and those who implement it" (1995, p. 219).

TJ does not restrict itself to a rights orientation. In addition, TJ examines whether proposed legal changes actually have their intended consequences (Wexler, 1991a). Thus, a TJ analysis might argue for procedural processes to be instituted not only on a constitutional basis but also on a therapeutic basis (see, for example, Tyler, 1992). This is not to say that a TJ assessment of therapeutic outcome should trump constitutional or other values (for example, Schopp, 1993; Wexler and Schopp, 1992), but rather that a TJ assessment provides additional information to be considered when making legal or policy judgments.

The TJ perspective *does not* argue that rights are unimportant. It *does not* argue that if a patient's constitutional rights have an antitherapeutic impact, then those rights (or other values) should be circumvented in order to facilitate therapeutic outcomes (see especially Schopp, 1993; Slobogin, 1995). It *does* argue that an examination of therapeutic implications is a valuable addition to the analysis of mental health law and policy, with potential benefits to individuals and to society at large.

To date, Therapeutic Jurisprudence has generated numerous empirical hypotheses regarding the salutary effects expected from various legal changes, although relatively little empirical data have been gathered by TJ researchers to verify these hypotheses (Schopp, 1995; Wexler and Winick, 1991; see also Slobogin, 1995; Wexler and Schopp, 1992). However, there are many researchers whose work is consistent with a TJ orientation. In the following discussion, the application of TJ and related research are considered in several specific areas of particular relevance to state psychiatric hospitals.

Consequences of Civil Commitment Hearings

Beginning in the 1970s, landmark Supreme Court decisions transformed the landscape of psychiatric hospitalization and defined the procedures, criteria, and standards for involuntary civil commitment and release (*Addington* v. *Texas,*

1978; *Heller* v. *Doe,* 1993; *O'Connor* v. *Donaldson,* 1975; *Parham* v. *J. R.,* 1979; *Zinermon* v. *Burch,* 1990; for another important legal analysis, see the opinion in the federal district court case of *Lessard* v. *Schmidt,* 1972). The consequences of these decisions were applications of legal safeguards to the civil commitment process. Since that time, civil commitment has come to be viewed as a quasi-criminal procedure in which a patient is guaranteed a due process hearing, representation by counsel, and a legal determination of the appropriateness of commitment (Melton, Petrila, Poythress, and Slobogin, 1997). The destination of a committed person is most often a state hospital.

Although patients' attitudes about civil commitment in general are varied (Edelsohn and Hiday, 1990; Hiday, 1988; Wood, Rosenthal, and Rodwon, 1984; Towes, El-Guebaly, and Leckie, 1981), TJ suggests that patients' perceptions of civil commitment hearings in particular can have a bearing on later psychiatric hospital treatment (see Wexler, 1991a). If the therapeutic and antitherapeutic consequences of civil commitment procedures can be pinpointed, then the means by which to handle these consequences in psychiatric hospitals can be better ascertained (see Tyler, 1992). For example, if research showed that clients who have difficult hearings are less compliant with treatment, then psychiatric hospital staff could anticipate perhaps greater levels of noncompliance and adjust their interventions accordingly. Thus, TJ recommends examining the civil commitment hearing as a psycholegal soft spot because of its potential impact on policy and procedure for clinical staff in psychiatric hospitals.

Tyler (1992) also suggests that patients' perceptions of the civil commitment hearing should be investigated as a psycholegal soft spot. He maintains that knowledge about how people are affected by judicial hearings generally can be applied to civil commitment hearings specifically. Tyler employs a conception of procedural justice and identifies three elements of legal procedure thought to be determinants of people's perceptions of procedural fairness—*participation, dignity,* and *trust.* According to Tyler, participants in the legal process perceive judicial procedures as fairer when they are permitted to participate more actively in court proceedings; they value the opportunity to become more involved and voice their arguments in court; they deem judicial procedures to be fairer when they are treated with respect and dignity; and they appear to be influenced by whether legal authorities show that they are concerned about the participant's welfare. Tyler argues that each of these findings has implications for civil commitment hearings and could potentially affect how patients view the process of hospitalization.

Involuntary Outpatient Commitment as a Discharge Alternative

Currently, statutory provisions exist for some form of *involuntary outpatient commitment* (IOC) in at least forty states (McCafferty and Dooley, 1990). IOC compels persons with mental illness who need treatment to submit to treatment on an outpatient basis either as an alternative to psychiatric hospitalization or after discharge from inpatient psychiatric facilities (for an overview, see Hiday, 1996). There are three types of IOC generally recognized. First, *outpatient commitment* is court-ordered treatment in the community and is usually characterized by short recurring visits to a mental health clinic that provides medication, individual or group therapy, day or partial-day programs, or supervision of living arrangements (King, 1995). Second, in *preventive commitment,* persons with long histories of hospitalizations and treatment noncompliance are discharged, but the commitment standard is lowered. If these individuals do not meet the civil commitment standard but still appear in need of treatment, they can be hospitalized (Stefan, 1987). Finally, with *conditional release,* patients are discharged to the community but are subject to behavioral requirements similar to those found in the inpatient milieu, such as abstaining from use of illicit substances, taking medications daily, or living in a supervised setting (Van Horn, 1994).

With respect to the psychiatric hospital, IOC represents a psycholegal soft spot that TJ recommends using for promoting therapeutic ends, particularly in the context of discharge. Although ethical, clinical, practical, and legal concerns about IOC still need to be addressed (see McCafferty and Dooley, 1990; Mulvey, Geller, and Roth, 1987), IOC may have certain advantages over traditional models of discharge, in which the legal relationship between the patient and the hospital is completely terminated after release (Bloom and Williams, 1994; Brakel, Parry, and Weiner, 1985). Used optimally, IOC would provide continuity of care beyond discharge, whereby risk of relapse or violence can be monitored in the community (Hiday, 1996). Outpatient treatment would allow for more effective responses by mental health providers to changes in patients' environment or mental status that precipitate relapse (Hinds, 1990). In addition, IOC would be consistent with the knowledge that slowly transitioning patients from the hospital is critical for treatment and would allow for adjustment to the community from inpatient hospital life (Bachrach, 1978; see also Stuve and Menditto, Chapter Three; and Sullivan, Chapter Four). Some forms of IOC may be the "only logical means of safely bridging the gap between hospital care and self-directed life in the community" (Brakel, Parry, and Weiner, 1985, p. 207).

Many people who could otherwise function in a community setting remain institutionalized because they do not participate in outpatient services (see Miller and Fiddleman, 1984). IOC can compel individuals to participate in treatment, which would especially be important for those who, without medications or psychosocial treatment, would predictably decompensate. Research has shown consistently that the use of outpatient services after discharge is associated with improved functioning and fewer admissions (see Hinds, 1990; see also Monroe-DeVita and Mohatt, Chapter Seven). IOC would ensure that outpatient services were utilized by individuals at risk, lowering readmissions overall. Legal mandates for appropriate outpatient services could also stimulate development and maintenance of such services. The sheer absence of community-based treatment and rehabilitation for state hospital residents has been a significant problem (see Stuve and Menditto, Chapter Three; Sullivan, Chapter Four; and Monroe-DeVita and Mohatt, Chapter Seven).

Empirical studies have not been conclusive as to whether IOC is an effective dispositional alternative (Maloy, 1996). However, several studies have shown that outpatient commitment and conditional release significantly reduce recidivism and relapse (Hiday and Scheid-Cook, 1991; Munetz, Grande, Kleist, and Peterson, 1995; reviewed by Hiday, 1996). Conditional release also has been determined to decrease recidivism and violent behavior of forensic patients in the community (Widerlanders, 1992). To date, there are no specific guidelines for IOC derived from the scientific literature on outcome of specific treatment or rehabilitation approaches (see Hiday, 1996; Maloy, 1996). The TJ perspective would be that for IOC to be reliably effective, it would have to be closely coordinated with specific approaches having known effectiveness.

Contingency management is a therapeutic approach with considerable potential for use in an IOC context. In contingency management, behavior is systematically modified through strategic use of reinforcers such as money, access to recreational resources, hospital privileges, and so forth. This approach is known to have powerful therapeutic benefits and is a key component in the overall effectiveness of psychiatric rehabilitation programs that effectively return the most severely disabled institutionalized individuals to community settings (see Paul and Lentz, 1977; Paul and Menditto, 1992; Liberman, 1992; Liberman and Bedell, 1989; Corrigan and Liberman, 1994). However, changes achieved in the institutional setting do not always generalize to community settings (see Corrigan, 1995), and this failure is often attributable to the fact that meaningful contingencies for reinforcing specific adaptive behaviors (or suppressing problem behaviors) cannot be "enforced" in a less controlled community-based setting.

Laws providing for conditional release may provide a partial solution to this problem. Adherence to a contingency management program could itself be a contingency in a conditional release agreement. The program would typically include reinforcers for continuing adherence to a comprehensive treatment and rehabilitation regimen, plus other contingencies for inhibiting problem behaviors. Case managers, residential supervisors, outpatient therapists, and family members could participate by monitoring target behaviors and providing reinforcers. The ultimate consequence of not adhering to the program would be rehospitalization, although with more intermediate consequences this would usually not be necessary.

Such an application of TJ is hypothesized to be therapeutic in a number of different ways. First, a period of conditional release can provide the patient with a smoother transition to the community and the sense that the hospital treatment is still available and present while the patient is in the community (Brakel, Parry, and Weiner, 1985). Second, the scheme provides an opportunity for generalization of skills learned from inpatient into outpatient settings.

Third, patient involvement in treatment planning can be fostered by incorporating patient input into the conditional release plans (Wexler, 1991c). Fourth, a provision for a follow-up evaluation can give the patient a feeling of accomplishment, of having lived independently for a certain amount of time outside the hospital setting (Schoenbaum, Cookson, and Stelovich, 1995). Fifth, the contingency of release revocation creates incentive for the patient to comply with treatment after release (see, for example, Widerlanders, 1992).

The Dangerousness Standard and Treatment Compliance

Involuntary civil commitment laws require a showing of mental illness plus dangerousness (*Addington* v. *Texas*, 1978). As a result, the assessment of present and future dangerousness, or *risk assessment,* constitutes a necessary and regular part of intake, treatment planning, and discharge decision making (see Scalora, Chapter Five). In the past, predictions of dangerousness have been viewed as problematic, on the grounds that clinicians are unable to predict violent or suicidal behavior with any reliability (Monahan, 1981). However, by the mid-1990s, a second and third generation of empirical research on risk assessment showed substantial improvement in appropriately trained clinicians' ability to predict violent behavior (Borum, 1996; Grisso and Tomkins, 1996; Monahan and Steadman, 1994; Monahan, 1997; Steadman and others, 1998; Lidz, Mulvey, and Gardner, 1993; Tardiff, 1998).

Several authors advocate the TJ principle of using dangerousness assessment as a therapeutic tool (Heilbrun, 1997; Wexler, 1991c; Beuford, McNeil, and Binder, 1997). If patients can become more involved in the risk evaluation itself, then patients' involvement in treatment can be fostered; thus, more compliance with treatment and aftercare planning in the long run can be encouraged. Models to promote patient involvement in discharge planning are not new (see, for example, Nightingale, 1990), and cognitive-behavioral therapy advocates this approach to counteract noncompliance (Miechenbaum and Turk, 1987).

Though empirical work has not been conducted yet to test specific hypotheses about treatment effects, patients' perceptions of their own engagement in treatment has been shown consistently to be related to treatment outcome and treatment compliance (Hiday, 1996; Kleinke, 1994; Miechenbaum and Turk, 1987). A recent empirical study showed that the quality of patients' therapeutic relationship with treatment providers was significantly related to their inpatient violent behavior (Beuford, McNeil, and Binder, 1997). At the very least, involving patients in risk evaluations does not appear to have antitherapeutic consequences (see Wexler, 1991c). The dangerousness standard for involuntary hospitalization is a psychologal soft spot that could potentially reap therapeutic benefits by engaging patients in their own risk assessments.

Informed Consent to Treatment and the Right to Refuse Medications

Informed consent has evolved considerably as a legal doctrine in the United States over the past thirty years. Case law has transformed informed consent from merely obtaining consent to *ensuring* that consent is informed (Behnke and Saks, 1998; Appelbaum, Lidz, and Meisel, 1987). An informed consent is defined as a decision that is made after the following information is provided to the patient or client—the nature and purpose of treatment; the risks and benefits of the treatment; the alternatives to treatment; and the risks and benefits of the alternatives, including no treatment at all. Consent to treatment is typically required at the outset of treatment (Kleinke, 1994).

From a TJ perspective, how informed consent is obtained can have strong therapeutic impact (Winick, 1997). Empirical literature on psychotherapy strongly supports the notion that establishing goals for psychotherapy contributes to treatment success (Kanfer and Gaelik-Buys, 1991). If this is the case, then the act of obtaining informed consent becomes a central component in therapists' attempts to achieve clinical gains with clients (Appelbaum, Lidz, and Meisel, 1987). Behnke and Saks (1998) propose that "obtaining informed consent is an interpersonal event that holds the potential to further, or inhibit, the patient's choices about the life she would like to live" (p. 967). The very process of negotiating and defining goals during this process can be therapeutic as well, providing the client a sense of ownership over the therapeutic process. Finally, treating patients in the psychiatric hospital as competent adults can foster alliance within the therapeutic relationship.

The right to refuse psychiatric medication is a subset of informed consent, but it has received separate attention in the law. Most recently, in *Riggins* v. *Nevada* (1992), the U.S. Supreme Court stated that involuntary administration of medication is a "substantial interference" with liberty interests protected by due process. However, the Court also held that forcing antipsychotic medications is permissible if there is a justification and determination of "medical appropriateness" and if there is no less intrusive means of treatment. Thus, the right to refuse medication is another psycholegal soft spot (Winick, 1997). As with informed consent in general, explicitly providing the patient an opportunity to consciously assert his or her right to refuse medications should itself be a therapeutic intervention. Systematically addressing the right to refuse medications in inpatient treatment should also foster therapeutic relationships between patients and staff.

Among the patients in state hospitals, there are many who are not competent to consent to treatment or who are compelled to take medication involuntarily under the circumstances identified by the Supreme Court. Overriding a patient's choices is never preferred, but when it is necessary, the process can be made maximally beneficial and minimally demoralizing by applying TJ principles. Formal processes for determining competence, appointing substitute decision makers, and justifying involuntary treatment regimens should include the patient's participation as much as possible. The goals of the process should include educating patients about what behaviors render them vulnerable to involuntary treatment and what behavioral changes could restore their competence or autonomy. Practitioners must be vigilant and even assertive in making sure that legal determinations about consent and related issues are clinically well informed and complete. In some cases, this may mean initiating actions with patients who are not competent to give informed consent, but who have not yet been recognized as such. From the TJ perspective, the therapeutic opportunity is not only in protecting the patient's rights but also in fully engaging the patient's collaboration in all relevant legal processes, regardless of their outcome.

The Future of Therapeutic Jurisprudence and the Psychiatric Hospital

So far, TJ scholarship has remained mainly in the province of academia, chiefly in the form of law reviews written by law school professors. The future of TJ will depend, in part, on collaborations with mental health researchers and practitioners to help determine what types of therapeutic goals are most important to achieve in different legal contexts. The impact of TJ on the role and operation of state psychiatric hospitals will depend on collaborations between legal scholars and practitioners and mental health researchers and practitioners (see Wexler, 1991a).

One immediate benefit of such a collaboration should be a general increase in mental health practitioners' familiarity and comfort with legal processes. Most mental health practitioners have minimal training in this area (see Melton, Petrila, Poythress, and Slobogin, 1997; Melton, Huss, and Tomkins, 1998). A modest improvement in this regard could have significant clinical impact. For example, an important reason involuntary outpatient commitment is not more widely utilized is that clinicians are not familiar with IOC statutes (see Hinds, 1990; Torrey and Kaplan, 1995). Better use of IOC could return state hospital patients to community settings more quickly and reduce the residual subpopulation of patients whose nonadherence to treatment necessitates long-term care in a highly restrictive setting.

A second benefit should be more appropriate and individualized management of treatment consent and refusal issues within the hospital. Involuntary psychiatric hospitalization itself has several legal objectives, only one of which is diagnosis and treatment (see Schopp, 1996). Protection of society and protection of patients' rights also are goals of involuntary hospitalization, but they are often at odds with each another. Sometimes one patient's rights (for example, to refuse treatment) leads to violation of other patients' rights (for example, to a safe and therapeutic environment). By framing psycholegal issues in therapeutic terms, TJ provides a perspective from which to view these often-competing values endemic in mental health treatment in hospitals. As such, clinicians can employ TJ to help sort through complicated issues that inevitably influence treatment decisions.

Finally, in the longer term, application of TJ should increase the effectiveness of specific treatment and rehabilitation modalities. There is already considerable conceptual, technical, and terminological overlap between TJ and important therapy approaches. For example, systematic attention to treatment consent and other decision-making issues are formal components of psychiatric rehabilitation counseling (Anthony and Liberman, 1986), contingency management, and *dialectical behavior therapy* (Linehan, 1993). All three of these modalities have known effectiveness for patients who are well represented in state hospitals and comparable settings. Collaborations with a TJ orientation should be expected to refine and extend such modalities, yielding better clinical outcome.

References

Addington v. *Texas,* 441 U.S. 418 (1978).

Anthony, W., and Liberman, R. "The Practice of Psychiatric Rehabilitation: Historical, Conceptual, and Research Base." *Schizophrenia Bulletin,* 1986, *12* (4), 542–559.

Appelbaum, P., Lidz, C., and Meisel, A. *Informed Consent: Legal Theory and Clinical Practice.* New York: Oxford University Press, 1987.

Bachrach, L. "A Conceptual Approach to Deinstitutionalization." *Hospital and Community Psychiatry,* 1978, *29,* 573–578.

Behnke, S., and Saks, E. "Therapeutic Jurisprudence: Informed Consent as a Clinical Indication for the Chronically Suicidal Patient with Borderline Personality Disorder." *Loyola of Los Angeles Law Review,* 1998, *31,* 945–981.

Beuford, J., McNeil, D., and Binder, R. "Utility of Initial Therapeutic Alliance in Evaluating Psychiatric Patients' Risk of Violence." *American Journal of Psychiatry,* 1997, *154,* 1272–1276.

Bloom, J., and Williams, M. *Management and Treatment of Insanity Acquittees: A Model for the 1990s.* Washington D.C.: American Psychiatric Press, 1994.

Borum, R. "Improving the Clinical Practice of Violence Risk Assessment." *American Psychologist,* 1996, *51,* 945–956.

Brakel, S., Parry, J., and Weiner, B. *The Mentally Disabled and the Law.* Chicago: American Bar Foundation, 1985.

Corrigan, P. "Use of Token Economy with Seriously Mentally Ill Patients: Criticisms and Misconceptions." *Psychiatric Services,* 1995, *46,* 1258–1263.

Corrigan, P., and Liberman, R. *Behavior Therapy in Psychiatric Hospitals.* New York: Springer, 1994.

Edelsohn, G. A., and Hiday, V. A. "Civil Commitment: A Range of Patient Attitiudes." *Bulletin of the American Academy of Psychiatry and Law,* 1990, *18,* 65–77.

Glendon, M. *Rights Talk: The Impoverishment of Political Discourse.* New York: Free Press, 1991.

Grisso, T., and Tomkins, A. "Communicating Violence Risk Assessments." *American Psychologist,* 1996, *51,* 928–930.

Heilbrun, K. "Prediction Versus Management Models Relevant to Risk Assessment: The Importance of Legal Decision-Making Context." *Law and Human Behavior,* 1997, *21,* 347–359.

Heller v. *Doe,* 113 S. Ct. 2637 (1993).

Hiday, V. "Civil Commitment: A Review of Empirical Research." *Behavioral Sciences and the Law,* 1988, *6,* 15–43

Hiday, V. "Outpatient Commitment: Official Coercion in the Community." In D. L. Dennis and J. Monahan (eds.), *Coercion and Aggressive Community Treatment: A New Frontier in Mental Health Law.* New York: Plenum, 1996.

Hiday, V., and Scheid-Cook, T. L. "Outpatient Commitment for 'Revolving Door' Patients: Compliance and Treatment." *Journal of Nervous and Mental Disease,* 1991, *179,* 83–88.
Hinds, J. "Involuntary Outpatient Commitment for the Chronically Mentally Ill." *Nebraska Law Review,* 1990, *69,* 346–412.
Kanfer, F., and Gaelik-Buys, L. "Self-Management Methods." In F. Kanfer and A. Goldstein (eds.), *Helping People Change.* New York: Pergamon Press, 1991.
Keilitz, I. "Justice and Mental Health Systems Interactions: An Overview and Introduction to the Special Issue." *Law and Human Behavior,* 1992, *16,* 1–4.
King, E. "Outpatient Civil Commitment in North Carolina: Constitutional and Policy Concerns." *Law and Contemporary Problems,* 1995, *58,* 251–281.
Kleinke, C. *Common Principles of Psychotherapy.* Pacific Grove, Calif.: Brooks/Cole, 1994.
Lessard v. *Schmidt,* 349 F. Suppl. (E.D. Wis. 1972).
Liberman. R. (ed.). *Handbook of Psychiatric Rehabilitation.* Old Tappan, N.J.: Macmillan, 1992.
Liberman, R., and Bedell, J. "Behavior Therapy." In H. Kaplan and B. Sadock (eds.), *Comprehensive Textbook of Psychiatry.* (5th ed.) Baltimore: Williams & Wilkins, 1989.
Lidz, C., Mulvey, E. and Gardner, W. "The Accuracy of Predictions of Violence to Others." *Journal of the American Medical Association,* 1993, *269,* 1007–1011.
Linehan, M. *Cognitive-Behavioral Treatment of Borderline Personality Disorder.* New York: Guilford Press, 1993.
Maloy, K. "Does Involuntary Outpatient Commitment Work?" In B. D. Sales and S. Shah (eds.), *Mental Health and Law: Research, Policy, and Services.* Durham, N.C.: Carolina Academic Press, 1996.
McCafferty, G., and Dooley, J. "Involuntary Outpatient Commitment: An Update." *Mental and Physical Disability Law Reporter,* 1990, *14,* 277–283.
Melton, G. B., Huss, M. T., and Tomkins, A. J. "Training in Psychology and Law. In I. Weiner and A. Hess (eds.), *Handbook of Forensic Psychology.* (2nd ed.) New York: Wiley, 1998, 700–720.
Melton, G., Petrila, J., Poythress, N., and Slobogin, C. *Psychological Evaluations for the Courts: A Handbook for Mental Health Professionals and Lawyers.* (2nd ed.) New York: Guilford Press, 1997.
Miechenbaum, D. and Turk, D. *Facilitating Treatment Adherence: A Practitioner's Guidebook.* New York: Plenum, 1987.
Miller, R. and Fiddleman, P. "Outpatient Commitment: Treatment in the Least Restrictive Alternative Environment?" *Hospital and Community Psychiatry,* 1984, *35,* 147–151.
Monahan, J. "The Clinical Prediction of Violent Behavior." Rockville, Md: National Institute of Mental Health, 1981.
Monahan, J. "Actuarial Support for the Clinical Assessment of Violence Risk." *International Review of Psychiatry,* 1997, *9,* 167–169.
Monahan, J., and Steadman, H. (eds.). *Violence and Mental Health: Developments in Risk Assessment.* Chicago: University of Chicago Press, 1994.
Mulvey, E., Geller, J., and Roth, L. "The Promise and Peril of Involuntary Outpatient Commitment." *American Psychologist,* 1987, *42,* 571–584.
Munetz, M., Grande, T., Kleist, J., and Peterson, G. "The Effectiveness of Outpatient Civil Commitment." *Psychiatric Services,* 1995, *47,* 1251–1253.
Nightingale, J. "Discharge Planning: Promoting Patient Involvement Through Group Process." *Social Work with Groups,* 1990, *13,* 83–94.
O'Connor v. *Donaldson,* 422 U.S. 563 (1975).
Parham v. *J. R.,* 442 U.S. 584 (1979).
Paul, G., and Lentz, R. *Psychosocial Treatment of Chronic Mental Patients: Milieu Versus Social-Learning Programs.* Cambridge, Mass.: Harvard University Press, 1977.
Paul, G., and Menditto, A. A. "Effectiveness of Inpatient Treatment Programs for Mentally Ill Adults in Public Psychiatric Facilities." *Applied and Preventive Psychology,* 1992, *1* (1), 41–63.

Perlin, M. *Mental Disability Law: Civil and Criminal.* Charlottesville, Va.: Michie, 1989.
Petrila, J. "Who Will Pay for Involuntary Civil Commitment Under Capitated Managed Care? An Emerging Dilemma." *Psychiatric Services,* 1995, *46* (10), 1045–1048.
Riggins v. *Nevada,* 504 U.S. 127 (1992).
Sales, B. (ed.). "Therapeutic Jurisprudence (Special Theme)." *Psychology, Public Policy, and Law,* 1995, *1* (1, entire issue).
Schoenbaum, S., Cookson, D., and Stelovich, S. "Postdischarge Follow-up of Psychiatric Inpatients and Readmission in an HMO Setting." *Psychiatric Services,* 1995, *46,* 943–945.
Schopp, R. "Therapeutic Jurisprudence and Conflicts Among Values in Mental Health Law." *Behavioral Sciences and the Law,* 1993, *11,* 31–45.
Schopp, R. "Sexual Predators and the Structure of the Mental Health System: Expanding the Normative Focus of Therapeutic Jurisprudence." *Psychology, Public Policy, and Law,* 1995, *1,* 161–192.
Schopp, R. "Communicating Risk Assessments: Accuracy, Efficacy, and Responsibility." *American Psychologist,* 1996, *51,* 939–944.
Shah, S. "Dangerousness: A Pardigm for Exploring Some Issues in Law and Psychology." *American Psychologist,* 1978, *33,* 224–238.
Slobogin, C. "Therapeutic Jurisprudence: Five Dilemmas to Ponder." *Psychology, Public Policy, and Law,* 1995, *1,* 193–219.
Steadman, H., and others. "Violence by People Discharged from Acute Psychiatric Inpatient Facilities and by Others in the Same Neighborhoods." *Archives of General Psychiatry,* 1998, *55,* 393–402.
Stefan, S. "Preventive Commitment: The Concept and Its Pitfalls." *Mental and Physical Law Reporter,* 1987, *11,* 288–296.
Symposium. "Psychological Jurisprudence: Another Perspective." *Southern Methodist University Law Review,* 1992, *46,* 323–445.
Symposium. "Therapeutic Jurisprudence: Restructuring Mental Disability Law." *New York Law School Journal of Human Rights,* 1993, *10,* 623–914.
Tardiff, K. "Prediction of Violence in Patients." *Journal of Practical Psychiatry and Behavioral Health,* 1998, *1,* 12–19.
Tomkins, A., and Carson, D. (eds.). "International Perspectives on Therapeutic Jurisprudence [special issue]." *Behavioral Sciences and the Law,* in press, *17* (4).
Torrey, E., and Kaplan, R. "A National Survey of the Use of Outpatient Commitment." *Psychiatric Services,* 1995, *46,* 778–784.
Towes, J., El-Guebaly, N., and Leckie, A. "Patients' Reactions to Their Commitment." *Canadian Journal of Psychiatry,* 1981, *26,* 251–254.
Tyler, T. "The Psychological Consequences of Judicial Proceedings: Implications for Civil Commitment Hearings." *Southern Methodist University Law Review,* 1992, *46,* 433–445.
Van Horn, P. "Revocation of Conditional Release in New York State: What Process Is Due?" *Columbia Journal of Law and Social Problems,* 1994, *27,* 523–556.
Wexler, D. (ed.). *Therapeutic Jurisprudence: The Law as a Therapeutic Agent.* Durham, N.C.: Carolina Academic Press, 1990.
Wexler, D. "An Introduction to Therapeutic Jurisprudence." In D. Wexler and B. Winick (eds.), *Essays in Therapeutic Jurisprudence.* Durham, N.C.: Carolina Academic Press, 1991a.
Wexler, D. "Putting Mental Health into Mental Health Law: Therapeutic Jurisprudence." In D. Wexler and B. Winick (eds.), *Essays in Therapeutic Jurisprudence.* Durham, N.C.: Carolina Academic Press, 1991b.
Wexler, D. "Health Care Compliance Principles and the Insanity Acquittee Conditional Release Process." *Criminal Law Bulletin,* 1991c, *27,* 18–41.
Wexler, D. "Putting Mental Health into Mental Health Law: Therapeutic Jurisprudence." *Law and Human Behavior,* 1992, *16,* 27–38.
Wexler, D. "Therapeutic Jurisprudence and Changing Conceptions of Legal Scholarship." *Behavioral Sciences and the Law,* 1993, *11,* 17–29.

Wexler, D. "Reflections on the Scope of Therapeutic Jurisprudence." *Psychology, Public Policy, and Law*, 1995, *1*, 230–236.

Wexler, D. "Practicing Therapeutic Jurisprudence: Psycholegal Soft Spots and Strategies." *Revista Jurídica Universidad de Puerto Rico*, 1998, *67*, 317–342.

Wexler, D., and Schopp, R. "Therapeutic Jurisprudence: A New Approach to Mental Health Law." In D. Kagehiro and W. Laufer (eds.), *Handbook of Psychology and Law*. New York: Springer-Verlag, 1992.

Wexler, D., and Winick, B. (eds.). *Essays in Therapeutic Jurisprudence*. Durham, N.C.: Carolina Academic Press, 1991.

Wexler, D., and Winick, B. (eds.). *Law in a Therapeutic Key: Developments in Therapeutic Jurisprudence*. Durham, N.C.: Carolina Academic Press, 1996.

Widerlanders, M. "Recidivism of Disordered Offenders Who Were Conditionally vs. Unconditionally Released." *Behavioral Sciences and the Law*, 1992, *10*, 141–148.

Winick, B. *The Right to Refuse Mental Health Treatment*. Washington D.C.: American Psychological Association, 1997.

Zinermon v. *Burch*, 494 U.S. 113 (1990).

Wood, K., Rosenthal, T., and Rodwon, K. "The Need for Hospitalization as Perceived by Emergency Room Patients and Clinicians." *Hospital and Community Psychiatry*, 1984, *35*, 830–832.

ERIC B. ELBOGEN is a graduate student in the Clinical Psychology Training Program and Law-Psychology Program at the University of Nebraska-Lincoln.

ALAN J. TOMKINS is director of the University of Nebraska Public Policy Center, professor in the Law-Psychology Program at the University of Nebraska-Lincoln, and editor of the journal Behavioral Sciences and the Law.

Assertive Community Treatment and related approaches will have a defining impact on state hospitals, now and in the future.

The State Hospital and the Community: An Essential Continuum for Persons with Severe and Persistent Mental Illness

Maria B. Monroe-DeVita, Dennis F. Mohatt

Three decades after the deinstitutionalization movement began, treatment, rehabilitation, and support for individuals with severe and persistent mental illness continue to shift from institutions to community-based agencies (National Association of State Mental Health Program Director, 1997). With this shift of focus has come the development of a variety of innovative community-based programs. Today, these programs serve many individuals who are at risk for state hospital admission as well as many previously served within the state hospital setting (Kuehnel, Liberman, Storzbach, and Rose, 1990; Soreff, 1996).

Historically, there has been debate about whether *all* state hospital functions can be transferred to the community (Bachrach, 1976; Bachrach, 1996). Though many suggest that the "state hospital versus community care" debate is now over (for example, Stein, 1992), calls for complete deinstitutionalization continue (for example, Kincheloe, 1997). Research thus far questions whether state hospitals can be downsized without increasing costs (Rothbard and others, 1998) or whether such closures can be completed at all (Fisher and others, 1996). As a result, it is imperative to examine the efficacy of community-based services, particularly for those individuals for whom state hospitals have been the primary source of services.

The authors wish to thank Deborah J. Allness, who provided feedback and guidance in the development of this chapter.

One of the most influential and widely researched community-based services is Assertive Community Treatment (ACT) (Drake and Burns, 1995), often described as a "hospital without walls." Studies have shown that ACT decreases hospital utilization among people with severe and disabling psychiatric disorders (Baronet and Gerber, 1998; Burns and Santos, 1995; Lehman, Steinwachs, and the Co-investigators of the Patient Outcomes Research Team Project, 1998; Marshall, 1997; Mueser, Bond, Drake, and Resnick, 1998; Olfson, 1990; Scott and Dixon, 1995a; Spollen, Meissler, and Santos, 1998; Test, 1992; Taube, Morlock, Burns, and Santos, 1990). Introduction and development of ACT has been associated with significant downsizing of state hospitals in several states, including Michigan, where ten-year statewide dissemination efforts corresponded with a reduction in nearly three thousand state hospital beds (Rutkowski and others, 1997; see also Scalora, Chapter Five).

This chapter is a critical analysis of ACT, its efficacy for persons who are at greatest risk for state hospital admission, and its impact on the state hospital system. ACT is not "all there is" to community-based services. It is the focus of this discussion because of the relatively large amount of research on its outcome and widespread interest among researchers, advocacy groups, and state program planners. Also, ACT is accessible to most mental health systems, due to the availability of implementation manuals, training materials, standards, and efforts to promote its implementation nationwide (Allness and Knoedler, 1998; Furlong-Norman, 1997; National Alliance for the Mentally Ill, 1998; Stein and Santos, 1998).

Background and Overview of ACT

Many community-based programs were developed in response to the unintended, pervasive, and negative outcomes of the first wave of deinstitutionalization—homelessness, incarceration, frequent incidents of relapse and readmission to state hospitals (that is, the "revolving-door" phenomenon), and transinstitutionalization (Stein, 1992; Torrey, Erdman, Wolfe, and Flynn, 1990). These consequences became quite visible by the early 1970s, supporting arguments that the Community Mental Health Centers Construction Act of 1963 did not bring about needed community services (Chu and Trotter, 1974).

In the early 1960s, researchers Arnold Marx, Leonard Stein, and Mary Ann Test found that despite the gains patients had made in a psychosocial inpatient program at Mendota State Hospital in Madison, Wisconsin, many were readmitted (Marx, Test, and Stein, 1973). A service model was developed to extend "hospital-like" services into the community. Over the course of subsequent development, the model was named the Total In-Community Treatment Team (Marx, Test, and Stein, 1973), Training in Community Living, and Program of Assertive Community Treatment (PACT) (Stein and Test, 1980; Test, 1992). The model has become most generally known as Assertive Community Treatment (ACT).

ACT consists of a comprehensive package of treatment, rehabilitation, and support services, addressing the full range of individuals' biopsychosocial needs in the community (Allness and Knoedler, 1998; Stein and Santos, 1998; Test, 1992). ACT services range from direct assistance with symptom management and instrumental functioning (for example, medication delivery and monitoring, assistance with shopping) and living-skills development (for example, living-skills training, vocational-skills training) to support with social casework issues (for example, securing Supplemental Security Income, obtaining adequate housing) and facilitating an optimally supportive environment (for example, family psychoeducation, social and leisure activities). Services are provided round-the-clock by an interdisciplinary team with a low staff-to-client ratio, typically one to ten. The ACT team is the primary provider of services, which it tailors to the needs of individual recipients. The majority of services are provided in vivo, in natural environments in the recipient's community. Services are not time limited. A recipient may require them indefinitely.

ACT services continue to evolve (Thompson, Griffith, and Leaf, 1990). Following a current trend to integrate psychosocial interventions into larger "service packages" (Scott and Dixon, 1995b), ACT incorporates specific treatment and rehabilitation modalities as they are developed and empirically validated (Allness and Knoedler, 1998; Stein and Santos, 1998).

The Heterogeneity of ACT. Despite the fact that ACT has been operationally defined and replicated in a variety of settings, the model has undergone adaptations and alterations in its fundamental principles, core services, and organizational structure. There is, therefore, some heterogeneity across programs that share the ACT label. Even in programs that adhere rigorously to the original model, individualization of services produces procedural heterogeneity.

Dissimilarities between programs multiply as they incorporate new treatment and rehabilitation modalities. For example, *social skills training* is commonly a component of an ACT program. In the outcome research that supports its efficacy, social skills training is an intensive and highly structured group therapy modality, requiring high levels of staff skill and client participation (Liberman, DeRisis, and Mueser, 1989). In some ACT programs, social skills training is provided according to this model, whereas in others, social skills training consists of semistructured social activities, such as going out for coffee.

Across the more than forty published studies, ACT models differ in a variety of respects (Mueser, Bond, Drake, and Resnick, 1998; Allness and Knoedler, 1998; Ridgely and others, 1996). A recent survey of 303 responding ACT programs in thirty-three states indicated that ACT models vary on such critical components as shared caseloads, twenty-four-hour service provision, time-unlimited services, and direct provision of services (Deci and others, 1995). For example, the Thresholds Bridge program in Chicago adapted ACT to their inner city–based psychosocial program, which currently *brokers* many services instead of directly providing them (Witheridge and Dincin,

1985). One of the cofounders of ACT describes a model that includes brokering services (Stein and Santos, 1998), a distinction from the model of another cofounder (Test, 1992), in which brokerage is a method of last resort. Program model "drift" has been observed internationally as well. For example, ACT teams in suburban Sydney, Australia, transfer their clients to less intensive services if they are clinically and functionally stable for over one year (Hambridge and Rosen, 1994).

Why ACT Programs Differ. ACT alterations occur in part because regions are socially, politically, and economically different, making exact replication of model programs difficult or impossible (Bachrach, 1988). For example, some communities have already invested in a variety of other community-based programs, such as psychosocial clubhouses and vocational rehabilitation. It may be good policy for ACT teams to broker such services instead of replicating them (Witheridge and Dincin, 1985). Similarly, elements of ACT, such as assertive outreach, lower caseloads, and service continuity have already been incorporated into some service systems (Essock, Drake, and Burns, 1998).

The recipient population also plays a critical role in the way ACT services are delivered. ACT was developed to serve the estimated 20 to 40 percent of persons with severe and persistent mental illness who are "in greatest need," as evidenced by significant *functional impairments* (for example, difficulty with maintaining daily personal hygiene, taking care of personal business affairs, maintaining employment) and *continuous high service needs* (for example, repeated psychiatric hospitalizations, psychiatric symptoms that have been treatment refractory, difficulty with engaging in traditional office-based services) (Allness and Knoedler, 1998). Even with such explicit criteria, persons in greatest need are a heterogeneous group, in terms of diagnosis, onset, course, symptomatology, level of severity, level of impairment, and service needs (Bachrach, 1993). For example, individuals who meet the continuous high service needs criteria due to difficulty in engaging in traditional mental health services may need more support services that specifically promote adherence and follow-up (for example, assertive outreach, multiple contacts per day), whereas those who meet such criteria based on treatment-refractory psychiatric symptoms may require more services addressing symptom management.

ACT is often adapted to serve particular subpopulations. These include homeless persons with severe and persistent mental illness (Dixon, Friedman, and Lehman, 1993; Dixon and others, 1995; Lehman and others, 1997), persons with comorbid mental illness and substance abuse problems (Drake and others, 1998; Drake, McHugo, and Noordsy, 1993; Teague, Drake, and Ackerson, 1995), Veterans Administration service recipients with mental illness (Neale and Rosenheck, 1995; Rosenheck and Neale, 1998), and homeless persons with mental illness released from jail (Solomon and Draine, 1995). Similarly, client characteristics may vary by location, further accounting for differential service needs (Burns and Santos, 1995). For example, homelessness and substance abuse may be more problematic for clients served in urban areas (Drake and others, 1997), whereas social isolation, poverty, stigma, and limited access to mental health services may be more problematic for clients served in rural areas (Mueser, Bond, Drake, and Resnick, 1998).

Geographical differences may also contribute to variations in ACT teams. For example, in rural areas, the long distances between towns and the lack of staff resources have essentially forced rural ACT teams to modify their service practices of providing twenty-four-hour coverage and a higher frequency of contacts (Fekete and others, 1998; Lachance and Santos, 1995; Santos and others, 1993).

Differing financing strategies and payment methods may also play a significant role in the extent to which particular ACT services are provided (Clark, 1997; Stein and Santos, 1998). Federal subsidies for ACT are more accessible for ACT-related services in states that include the Psychosocial Rehabilitation Option in their Medicaid plan (Allness and Knoedler, 1998; Mowbray, Plum, and Masterton, 1997; Stein and Santos, 1998) than in states that are limited to the Clinic Option. *Retrospective financing mechanisms* (for example, fee-for-service) allow for better monitoring of services actually provided, but may inhibit availability of services that generate less revenue. *Prospective financing* (for example, per diem) allows some flexibility in the services provided, but with greater difficulty in pinpointing which services were actually delivered (Clark, 1997).

Several states may have altered ACT to maximize perceived cost-effectiveness (Burns and Santos, 1995), especially states that contract with managed care organizations to provide mental health services. A profit-oriented managed care perspective emphasizes use of specific services that provide the best outcome at the lowest cost in a limited time frame, rather than investment in a service *model* whose benefits may accrue more slowly (Steinwachs and others, 1997).

ACT Outcome Research

The various sources of heterogeneity in ACT produce inconsistencies in the results of outcome research. Careful analysis of heterogeneity across ACT programs is necessary in interpreting the research data. Similarly, it is increasingly important to identify the particular components of ACT that contribute to its overall outcome (Spollen, Meissler, and Santos, 1998). Several studies have identified such elements (for example, in vivo service delivery, low staff-to-client ratio, shared caseloads) (Lachance and Santos, 1995; McGrew and Bond, 1995; Witheridge, 1991). Researchers have developed measures of program fidelity (McGrew, Bond, Dietzen, and Salyers, 1994; Teague, Drake, Ackerson, 1995; Teague, Drake, and Bond, 1995) and methods of documenting the actual services provided by ACT teams (for example, Brekke and Test, 1987). One study found that programs that adhered most closely to the original model had lower hospital utilization (McGrew, Bond, Dietzen, and Salyers, 1994). Unfortunately, however, much of the research on ACT has not included scrupulous attention to the content or procedural fidelity of its specific treatment and rehabilitation modalities, and access to such information is seriously limited. Until this methodological limitation is addressed, conclusions from the research remain incomplete.

The original ACT program in Madison, Wisconsin, continues to find the most consistent and positive client outcomes across a variety of domains (Stein and Test, 1980; Test and others, 1994). The first ACT outcome study targeted an unselected group of persons presenting for state hospital admission (half of whom were diagnosed with schizophrenia) (Stein and Test, 1980), whereas the second ongoing longitudinal study focuses on young adults with recent onset of schizophrenia, schizoaffective disorder, or schizotypal personality disorder, with a history of fewer than twelve months in psychiatric hospitals or penal institutions (Test, 1992). The first study compared ACT to standard hospital and aftercare services, whereas the second study continues to compare ACT to the range of services provided within the local mental health system in Madison.

Taken together, the results of these studies suggest that in comparison with the control group, ACT clients spent less time in psychiatric hospitals, skilled nursing facilities, legal settings, and in homeless conditions; spent more time in independent living and demonstrated greater success in that setting; spent less time unemployed, more time in sheltered employment, more time in normative employment, and earned more income from competitive employment; demonstrated less psychiatric symptomatology and less subjective distress; reported greater satisfaction with life; demonstrated better medication compliance eight and sixteen months after admission; reported more contact with trusted friends and participation in social groups; and demonstrated no greater family or community burden (Stein and Test, 1980; Test and others, 1994). There were no significant differences found between the ACT clients and control groups in their level of suicidality, ability to maintain social relationships, leisure-time activities, and quality of environment (Stein and Test, 1980; Test and others, 1994).

ACT's effectiveness in reducing psychiatric hospital utilization is a strong and consistent finding, particularly for those individuals who are high service users (Baronet and Gerber, 1998; Burns and Santos, 1995; Lehman, Steinwachs, and the Co-investigators of the Patient Outcomes Research Team Project, 1998; Marshall, 1997; Mueser, Bond, Drake, and Resnick, 1998; Olfson, 1990; Scott and Dixon, 1995a; Spollen, Meissler, and Santos, 1998; Test, 1992; Taube, Morlock, Burns, and Santos, 1990). In most reviews and in one empirical meta-analysis (Marshall, 1997), ACT was also consistently found to improve housing stability and level of independent living (Baronet and Gerber, 1998; Burns and Santos, 1995; Marshall, 1997; Mueser, Bond, Drake, and Resnick, 1998; Scott and Dixon, 1995a), as well as client and family satisfaction (Baronet and Gerber, 1998; Burns and Santos, 1995; Marshall, 1997; Mueser, Bond, Drake, and Resnick, 1998; Olfson, 1990; Test, 1992).

ACT's impact on psychiatric symptoms, employment, social functioning, and quality of life has been less consistently supported. Some reviews indicate a significant reduction in psychiatric symptoms (Baronet and Gerber, 1998; Scott and Dixon, 1995a; Taube, Morlock, Burns and Santos, 1990; Test, 1992), whereas others suggest more modest effects (Mueser, Bond, Drake, and Resnick, 1998), and still others indicate mixed results or no significant findings (Burns and Santos, 1995; Marshall, 1997; Olfson, 1990; Spollen, Meissler, and Santos, 1998; Test, 1992). Some indicate that ACT clients spend significantly more time employed (Marshall, 1997; Taube, Morlock, Burns, and Santos, 1990), but others indicate little effect (Mueser, Bond, Drake, and Resnick, 1998), or mixed outcomes (Baronet and Gerber, 1998; Burns and Santos, 1995; Spollen, Meissler, and Santos, 1998; Test, 1992), or no effect (Olfson, 1990). Social functioning has been more variably measured in the literature. Two reviews found ACT to have a significantly positive impact on social functioning (Scott and Dixon, 1995a; Taube, Morlock, Burns, and Santos, 1990), one review found little effect (Mueser, Bond, Drake, and Resnick, 1998), three indicated mixed findings (Burns and Santos, 1995; Spollen, Meissler, and Santos, 1998; Test, 1992), and two indicated no impact (Marshall, 1997; Olfson, 1990). Only one review found moderate improvements in quality of life (Mueser, Bond, Drake, and Resnick, 1998), whereas most reviews indicated mixed results or no effect at all (Baronet and Gerber, 1998; Olfson, 1990; Scott and Dixon, 1995a; Spollen, Meissler, and Santos, 1998; Test, 1992). Outcome in areas such as program retention, medication and treatment compliance, jail time, substance abuse, and family burden have not been consistently examined across research studies.

Several studies have examined the extent to which ACT clients can be transferred to less intensive community-based services over time (McRae, Higgins, Lycan, and Sherman, 1990; Salyers and others, 1998; Stein and Test, 1980). Overall, findings have been mixed, but several hypotheses may be drawn from them. ACT clients who are high service users may not fare well with a step-down approach, however. Such a transfer may be possible for ACT clients who have become relatively low service users and have made significant gains in independent functioning (Mueser, Bond, Drake, and Resnick, 1998; see Salyers and others, 1998).

Cost-effectiveness and cost-benefit studies of ACT have also been inconsistent. The original ACT study found that ACT had a small economic advantage over hospital-based care (Weisbrod, Test, and Stein, 1980). Several subsequent reviews and studies comparing ACT to other community-based services have found ACT to be cost-effective for individuals who are high users of hospital services (Essock, Frisman, and Kontos, 1998; Taube, Morlock, Burns, and Santos, 1990). However, in studies that assessed ACT in comparison to more rigorous community-based services for clients who were not high users of hospital services, ACT was no more cost-effective (Drake and others, 1998).

The inconsistencies in the ACT outcome research may be due in part to use of different outcome measures and outcome indicators (Burns and Santos,

1995; Taube, Morlock, Burns, and Santos, 1990), varying time periods for treatment and assessment (Burns and Santos, 1995; Olfson, 1990), and general methodological differences (McHugo and others, 1998). However, it seems unlikely that this can account for all the differences. In view of the heterogeneity of ACT and its recipient populations, logic points to two nonmutually exclusive conclusions: some kinds of ACT (as defined by core services, organizational structure, and so forth) are better than others; and ACT is more beneficial for some recipients than for others. This recalls Gordon Paul's famous comment that outcome research ultimately needs to go beyond global hypotheses of efficacy to determine, "What treatment, by whom, is most effective for this individual with what specific problem, under which circumstances, and how does it come about?" (Paul, 1969, p. 44). ACT research has only just begun to address these questions.

In this context, policy issues that look beyond the most basic principles (for example, mental health systems should have the capability of providing ACT) can be only tentatively addressed. Questions as to whether recipients can or should be moved to less intensive programs, whether high service use should be an eligibility criterion, what variables produce optimum cost-effectiveness, or even who can be safely and effectively served cannot be confidently answered based on current research findings. The relative contribution of ACT as a unified approach, as opposed to specific *components* of ACT delivered in other ways, is unclear. ACT services have been implemented to varying degrees, along with a variety of other supports and services, including case management, emergency services, residential facilities, and subacute hospitalization (for example, Rothbard, Richman, and Hadley, 1997; Rothbard and others, 1998). Comprehensive service arrays that lack the unifying and coordinating aspects of ACT may not optimally reduce hospitalization.

Future research needs to examine outcomes systematically across a variety of domains and variables, including those that are client-, setting-, and service-specific (Paul and Menditto, 1992). Continued efforts toward examining essential elements and direct-service practices will further aid this process and will be necessary to fully understand the outcome data. This does not mean that promotional activities and other efforts to stimulate development of ACT capability are ill-advised or premature, but it does indicate caution in mental health system planning regarding expectations about the nature and universality of ACT's benefits.

Implications for the State Hospital

Despite the ambiguities in the research, it is clear that at the very least, ACT has made it possible for many persons with severe and persistent mental illness to live in community settings. In all probability, ACT will continue to be a factor in state hospital downsizing efforts. ACT not only reduces the need for long-term hospitalization but also enables recipients to use shorter-term inpatient services that are more commonly available in the private sector.

Ultimately, however, more must be learned about the particular nature of ACT "successes" and "failures" to predict its final impact on the role of state hospitals. There is some agreement that ACT is not successful for some individuals (Mueser, Bond, Drake, and Resnick, 1998). Even in Stein and Test's (1980) widely cited original ACT study, about 18 percent were rehospitalized (see Allness and Knoedler, 1998). There have been no systematic studies of the characteristics of unsuccessful ACT recipients. It is probably a heterogeneous group. Many factors may contribute to failure, including the sheer severity of disability, persistence of acute psychosis, presence of high-risk behaviors and active noncompliance. Until more is known about this, an appropriate principle for mental health services planning would seem to be that ACT programs should be expected to successfully serve about 80 to 85 percent of the traditional state hospital recipient population. Alternatives must be available for the 15 to 20 percent for whom ACT fails. State hospitals may play an important role in this regard.

The evidence that ACT actually improves personal and social functioning is inconsistent. The evidence that it improves quality of life is weak at best. ACT's emphasis on extraordinary support, as opposed to functional improvement, even raises concerns that it fosters dependency (Estroff, 1981). Although reducing hospital utilization is an intrinsically worthwhile goal, policy dilemmas arise if extraordinary support is an *alternative* to functional recovery. Ironically, some of the strongest empirical support for the efficacy of psychosocial rehabilitation in improving patients' functioning comes from Paul and Lentz's (1977) landmark outcome study, conducted in long-term inpatient settings (see also Stuve and Menditto, Chapter Three). It is possible that at least for some individuals, functional recovery requires services and settings more intensive than those typically associated with ACT, at least during discrete periods of time. If so, this may suggest an important role for state hospitals of the future.

Conclusions

The extent to which ACT and related technologies will affect the role and recipient population of state hospitals is unclear. Key parameters are indeterminate or remain unknown, including the characteristics of successful recipients and their representation in the overall population, the nature of failure cases, the role of consent and involuntary treatment, the degree to which true rehabilitation is part of the ACT program, and the results of the cost-effectiveness calculus that considers the long-term value of functional improvement in comparison to continuing extraordinary support. Nevertheless, further ACT dissemination must be expected to contribute to a transformation of state hospital populations, toward smaller numbers of individuals who have more severe disorders and disabilities, and higher levels of noncompliance and dangerousness. This indicates a need for differentiation of function between the state hospital and the community, with state hospitals specializing in the unique needs of that subpopulation.

With modern rehabilitation technology, it can be expected that most individuals who need state hospital–based services that provide such rehabilitation at one point in time will achieve enough functional recovery to move on to community-based services. State hospitals and community-based agencies should provide a continuum of rehabilitation services to reflect that expectation. Active collaboration and exchange of resources and technologies between rehabilitation programs, regardless of their settings, are necessary for an optimal continuum of services (see Vandiver, 1997). In particular, future state hospital downsizing efforts should focus on application of rehabilitation technology *across the entire service system* and on the need for greater communication and service coordination between various settings.

References

Allness, D., and Knoedler, W. *The PACT* [Program of Assertive Community Treatment] *Model of Community-Based Treatment for Persons with Severe and Persistent Mental Illnesses: A Manual for PACT Start-up.* Arlington, Va.: National Alliance for the Mentally Ill, 1998.

Bachrach, L. *Deinstitutionalization: An Analytical Review and Sociological Perspective.* Rockville, Md.: National Institute of Mental Health, 1976.

Bachrach, L. "On Exporting and Importing Model Programs." *Hospital and Community Psychiatry,* 1988, *39 (12),* 1257–1258.

Bachrach, L. "The Biopsychosocial Legacy of Deinstitutionalization." *Hospital and Community Psychiatry,* 1993, *44,* 523–524, 526.

Bachrach, L. "The State of the State Hospital in 1996." *Psychiatric Services,* 1996, *47* (10), 1071–1078.

Baronet, A., and Gerber, G. "Psychiatric Rehabilitation: Efficacy of Four Models." *Clinical Psychology Review,* 1998, *18,* 189–228.

Brekke, J., and Test, M. "An Empirical Analysis of Services Delivered in a Model Community Support Program." *Psychosocial Rehabilitation Journal,* 1987, *10* (4), 51–61.

Burns, B., and Santos, A. "Assertive Community Treatment: An Update of Randomized Trials." *Psychiatric Services,* 1995, *46,* 669–675.

Chu, F., and Trotter, S. *The Madness Establishment: Ralph Nader's Study Group Report on the National Institute of Mental Health.* Old Tappan, N.J.: Grossman, 1974.

Clark. R. "Financing Assertive Community Treatment." *Administration and Policy in Mental Health,* 1997, *25* (2), 209–219.

Deci, P., and others. "Dissemination of Assertive Community Treatment Programs." *Psychiatric Services,* 1995, *46,* 676–678.

Dixon, L., Friedman, N., and Lehman, A. "Compliance of Homeless Mentally Ill Persons with Assertive Community Treatment." *Hospital and Community Psychiatry,* 1993, *44* (6), 581–583.

Dixon, L., and others. "Modifying the PACT Model to Serve Homeless Persons with Severe Mental Illness." *Psychiatric Services,* 1995, *46* (7), 684–688.

Drake, R., and Burns, B. "Special Section on Assertive Community Treatment: An Introduction." *Psychiatric Services,* 1995, *46,* 667–678.

Drake, R., McHugo, G., and Noordsy, D. "Treatment of Alcoholism Among Schizophrenic Outpatients: Four-Year Outcomes." *American Journal of Psychiatry,* 1993, *150,* 328–329.

Drake, R., and others. "Integrated Treatment for Dually Diagnosed Homeless Adults." *Journal of Nervous and Mental Disease,* 1997, *185,* 298–305.

Drake, R., and others. "Assertive Community Treatment for Patients with Co-occurring Severe Mental Illness and Substance Use Disorder: A Clinical Trial." *American Journal of Orthopsychiatry,* 1998, *68* (2), 201–215.

Essock, S., Drake, R., and Burns, B. "A Research Network to Evaluate Assertive Community Treatment: Introduction." *American Journal of Orthopsychiatry,* 1998, *68* (2), 176–178.

Essock, S., Frisman, L. and Kontos, N. "Cost-Effectiveness of Assertive Community Treatment Teams." *American Journal of Orthopsychiatry,* 1998, *68* (2), 179–190.

Estroff, S. *Making It Crazy: An Ethnographic Study of Psychiatric Clients in an American Community.* Berkeley: University of California Press, 1981.

Fekete, D., and others. "Rural Assertive Community Treatment: A Field Experiment." *Psychiatric Rehabilitation Journal,* 1998, *21* (4), 371–379.

Fisher, W., and others. "Case Mix in the 'Downsizing' State Hospital." *Psychiatric Services,* 1996, *47* (3), 255–262.

Furlong-Norman, K. "From the Editor." *Community Support Network News,* 1997, *11* (4), 2.

Hambridge, J., and Rosen, A. "Assertive Community Treatment for the Seriously Mentally Ill in Suburban Sydney: A Programme Description and Evaluation." *Australian and New Zealand Journal of Psychiatry,* 1994, *28,* 438–445.

Kincheloe, M. "A State Mental Health System with No State Hospital: The Vermont Plan Ten Years Later." *Psychiatric Services,* 1997, *48* (8), 1078–1080.

Kuehnel, T., Liberman, R., Storzbach, D., and Rose, G. *Resource Book for Psychiatric Rehabilitation: Elements of Service for the Mentally Ill.* Baltimore: Williams & Wilkins, 1990.

Lachance, K., and Santos, A. "Modifying the PACT Model: Preserving Critical Elements." *Psychiatric Services,* 1995, *46,* 601–604.

Lehman, A. F, Steinwachs, D., and the Co-investigators of the Patient Outcomes Research Team Project. "Translating Research into Practice: The Schizophrenia Patient Outcomes Research Team Treatment Recommendations." *Schizophrenia Bulletin,* 1998, *24,* 1–10.

Lehman, A., and others. "A Randomized Trial of Assertive Community Treatment for Homeless Persons with Severe Mental Illness." *Archives of General Psychiatry,* 1997, *54,* 1038–1043.

Liberman, R., DeRisis, W., and Mueser, K. *Social Skills Training for Psychiatric Patients.* Needham Heights, Mass.: Allyn & Bacon, 1989.

Marshall, M. *Systematic Review of the Effectiveness of Case Management and Assertive Community Treatment for People with Severe Mental Disorders.* Unpublished manuscript, 1997.

Marx, A., Test, M., and Stein, L. "Extrohospital Management of Severe Mental Illness." *Archives of General Psychiatry,* 1973, *29,* 505–511.

McGrew, J., and Bond, G. "Critical Ingredients of Assertive Community Treatment: Judgments of the Experts." *Journal of Mental Health Administration,* 1995, *22* (2), 113–125.

McGrew, J., Bond, G., Dietzen, L., and Salyers, M. "Measuring the Fidelity of Implementation of a Mental Health Program Model." *Journal of Consulting and Clinical Psychology,* 1994, *62* (4), 670–678.

McHugo, G., and others. "Methodological Issues in Assertive Community Treatment Studies." *American Journal of Orthopsychiatry,* 1998, *68* (2), 246–260.

McRae, J., Higgins, M., Lycan, C., and Sherman, W. "What Happens to Patients After Five Years of Intensive Case Management Stops?" *Hospital and Community Psychiatry,* 1990, *41,* 175–179.

Mowbray, C., Plum, T., and Masterton, T. "Harbinger II: Deployment and Evolution of Assertive Community Treatment in Michigan." *Administration and Policy in Mental Health,* 1997, *25* (2), 125–139.

Mueser, K., Bond, G., Drake, R., and Resnick, S. "Models of Community Care for Severe Mental Illness: A Review of Research on Case Management." *Schizophrenia Bulletin,* 1998, *24,* 37–73.

National Alliance for the Mentally Ill. *Falling Through the Cracks: The Nation's Continued Failure to Provide Care and Treatment for Individuals with the Most Severe Mental Illness.* Arlington, Va.: National Alliance for the Mentally Ill, Oct. 1998.

National Association of State Mental Health Program Directors. *Closing and Reorganizing State Psychiatric Hospitals: 1996.* State Mental Health Agency Profile System Highlights, no. 1. Alexandria, Va.: National Association of State Mental Health Program Directors, Dec. 1997.

Neale, M., and Rosenheck, R. "Therapeutic Alliance and Outcome in a Veterans Administration Intensive Case Management Program." *Psychiatric Services,* 1995, *46,* 719–721.

Olfson, M. "Assertive Community Treatment: An Evaluation of the Experimental Evidence." *Hospital and Community Psychiatry,* 1990, *41,* 634–641.

Paul, G. "Behavior Modification Research: Design and Tactics." In C. Franks (ed.), *Behavior Therapy: Appraisal and Status.* New York: McGraw-Hill, 1969.

Paul, G., and Lentz, R. *Psychosocial Treatment of Chronic Mental Patients: Milieu Versus Social-Learning Programs.* Cambridge, Mass.: Harvard University Press, 1977.

Paul, G., and Menditto, A. A. "Effectiveness of Inpatient Treatment Programs for Mentally Ill Adults in Public Psychiatric Facilities." *Applied and Preventive Psychology,* 1992, *1* (1), 41–63.

Ridgely, S., and others. "Characteristics and Activities of Case Managers in the Robert Wood Johnson Foundation Program on Chronic Mental Illness." *Psychiatric Services,* 1996, *47* (7), 737–743.

Rosenheck, R., and Neale, M. "Intersite Variation in the Impact of Intensive Psychiatric Community Care on Hospital Use." *American Journal of Orthopsychiatry,* 1998, *68* (2), 191–200.

Rothbard, A., Richman, E., and Hadley, T. "Unbundling of State Hospital Services in the Community: The Philadelphia State Hospital Story." *Administration and Policy in Mental Health,* 1997, *24,* 391–398.

Rothbard, A., and others. "Cost Comparison of State Hospital and Community-Based Care for Seriously Mentally Ill Adults." *American Journal of Psychiatry,* 1998, *155* (4), 523–529.

Rutkowski, P., and others. "PACT Dissemination and Implementation from Three States and the Department of Veterans Affairs." *Community Support Network News,* 1997, *11* (4), 8–9.

Salyers, M., and others. "Transferring Clients from Intensive Case Management: Impact on Client Functioning." *American Journal of Orthopsychiatry,* 1998, *68* (2), 233–245.

Santos, A., and others. "Providing Assertive Community Treatment for Severely Mentally Ill Patients in a Rural Area." *Hospital and Community Psychiatry,* 1993, *44* (1), 34–39.

Scott, J., and Dixon, L. "Assertive Community Treatment and Case Management for Schizophrenia." *Schizophrenia Bulletin,* 1995a, *21* (4), 657–668.

Scott, J., and Dixon, L. "Psychological Interventions for Schizophrenia." *Schizophrenia Bulletin,* 1995b, *21* (4), 621–630.

Solomon, P., and Draine, J. "Jail Recidivism in a Forensic Case Management Program." *Health and Social Work,* 1995, *20,* 167–173.

Soreff, S. (ed.). *Handbook for the Treatment of the Seriously Mentally Ill.* Seattle: Hogrefe & Huber, 1996.

Spollen, J., Meissler, N., and Santos, A. "Assertive Community Treatment." *Journal of Practical Psychiatry and Behavioral Health,* 1998, *4,* 102–109.

Stein, L. "Editor's Notes." In L. Stein (ed.), *Innovative Community Mental Health Programs.* New Directions for Mental Health Services, no. 56. San Francisco: Jossey-Bass, 1992.

Stein, L., and Santos, A. *Assertive Community Treatment of Persons with Severe Mental Illness.* New York: Norton, 1998.

Stein, L., and Test, M. "Alternative to Mental Hospital Treatment." *Archives of General Psychiatry,* 1980, *37,* 392–397.

Steinwachs, D., and others. "Experiences with Managed Care and PACT." *Community Support Network News,* 1997, *11* (4), 14–16.

Taube, C., Morlock, L., Burns, B., and Santos, A. "New Directions in Research on Assertive Community Treatment." *Hospital and Community Psychiatry,* 1990, *41,* 642–647.

Teague, G., Drake, R., and Ackerson, T. "Evaluating Use of Continuous Treatment Teams for Persons with Mental Illness and Substance Abuse." *Psychiatric Services,* 1995, *46,* 689–695.

Teague, G., Drake, R., and Bond, G. "The Dartmouth Assertive Community Treatment Fidelity Scale." Unpublished scale. Lebanon: New Hampshire-Dartmouth Psychiatric

Research Center, 1995.

Test, M. "Training in Community Living." In R. Liberman (ed.), *Handbook of Psychiatric Rehabilitation.* Old Tappan, N.J.: Macmillan, 1992.

Test, M., and others. "Long-Term Care of Schizophrenia: Seven Year Results." Paper presented at the annual meeting of the American Psychiatric Association, Philadelphia, May 1994.

Thompson, K., Griffith, E., and Leaf, P. "A Historical Review of the Madison Model of Community Care." *Hospital and Community Psychiatry,* 1990, *41,* 625–634.

Torrey, E., Erdman, K., Wolfe, S., and Flynn, L. *Care of the Seriously Mentally Ill: A Rating of State Programs.* (3rd ed.) Washington, D.C.: Public Citizen Health Research Group and the National Alliance for the Mentally Ill, 1990.

Vandiver, V. "Institutional and Community Approaches to the Provision of Mental Health Services." In T. Watkins and J. Callicutt (eds.), *Mental Health Policy and Practice Today.* Thousand Oaks, Calif.: Sage, 1997.

Weisbrod, B., Test, M., and Stein, L. "Alternative to Mental Hospital Treatment, III: Economic Benefit-Cost Analysis." *Archives of General Psychiatry,* 1980, *37,* 400–405.

Witheridge, T. "The 'Active Ingredients' of Assertive Outreach." In. N. Cohen (ed.), *Psychiatric Outreach to the Mentally Ill.* New Directions for Mental Health Services, no. 52. San Francisco: Jossey-Bass, 1991.

Witheridge, T, and Dincin, J. "The Bridge: An Assertive Outreach Program in an Urban Setting." In L. Stein and M. A. Test (eds.), *The Training in Community Model: A Decade of Experience.* New Directions for Mental Health Services, no. 26. San Francisco: Jossey-Bass, 1985.

MARIA B. MONROE-DEVITA is a graduate student in the Clinical Psychology Training Program at the University of Nebraska-Lincoln and served as team leader in the development of a statewide program evaluation of Assertive Community Treatment in Nebraska.

DENNIS F. MOHATT is western regional vice president for Alternative Behavioral Services and former deputy director of the Nebraska Department of Health and Human Services, where he served as commissioner of mental health.

Computerized data management technology for clinical decision making is a key to optimizing the performance of programs serving the most severely disabled and treatment-resistant patients.

Clinical Decision Support Systems in State Hospitals

Brett Buican, William D. Spaulding, Bruce Gordon, Toni Hindman

In the twenty-first century, state hospitals will be required to develop more sophisticated methods of managing and utilizing clinical data. The impetus for this development will include mandates from accrediting agencies and managed care companies. For example, the Joint Commission on Accreditation of Healthcare Organizations (JCAHO) is now requiring that all health care organizations adopt performance measurement systems. According to JCAHO, these systems will provide "scientifically valid, data-driven mechanisms that generate a continuous stream of performance information enabling organizations to . . . support their claims of quality . . . receive early warning of problems . . . verify the effectiveness of corrective actions . . . identify areas of excellence . . . and compare their performance with that of peer organizations" (1998, p. 1). Thus, outcome data will increasingly serve an accountability, program evaluation, and benchmarking role in coming years.

The growing recognition that clinical data management is an important component in quality improvement, policy development, managed care, and related administrative functions has already produced a market for computer application packages dedicated to these purposes. State mental health administrations have begun to develop systems for collecting and analyzing data from multiple institutions and agencies (for example, Bigelow, 1989). JCAHO has developed criteria for approving such packages as part of the accreditation process. Applications now available on the software market are generally suitable for the kind of data management that administrative uses entail, in some cases even including software for formatting individual patients' treatment plans. However, there is another crucial type of data management application having special importance to the roles and recipient populations of state hospitals—data management as a *Clinical Decision Support System*[1] (CDSS). Systems optimized for administrative purposes cannot be expected to function optimally for this application. A CDSS functions primarily to inform an individual patient's treatment team about the patient's clinical status, response to treatments, and progress in rehabilitation. Of course, these kind of data also have administrative uses, but a CDSS must manage more detailed data, with a much faster turnaround between collection and formatted output, than is the case for the administrative context. The data in a CDSS must be routinely available to clinicians, virtually on a moment's notice, as clinical assessment issues arise and are addressed with intervention decisions. In order to fully realize the benefits of state-of-the-art treatment technology and achieve maximal cost-effectiveness, state hospitals and comparable institutions and agencies of the future will need *both* administrative data management and CDSS capabilities. The purpose of this chapter is to characterize the functions and design prerequisites of a CDSS for application in state hospitals.

Why a Clinical Decision Support System Is Necessary in State Hospitals

There have been pioneering efforts to develop CDSS systems for state hospitals and comparable settings (for example, Paul, 1986; Spaulding, Crinean, and Martin, 1983; Spaulding, Hargrove, Crinean, and Martin, 1981). However, the rapid and complex evolution of new treatment and rehabilitation technologies creates a "moving target." Data management demands change as new assessment instruments and treatment modalities become available. Any discussion of a CDSS for state hospitals is, to a significant degree, a "snapshot in time." However, there are some enduring principles that when considered in the context of current technology can guide development of CDSS systems into the foreseeable future.

The primary function of a Clinical Decision Support System is to effectively manage clinical data to facilitate clinical decision making. A CDSS achieves this function by organizing and summarizing clinical data and then returning these data to treatment teams in a readily interpretable format for use in day-to-day clinical activities.

The data management functions of a CDSS are increasingly important for several reasons. First, as mental health reform attempts to cut costs, the recipient population at state hospitals will increasingly be the most disabled and treatment resistant (see Monroe-DeVita and Mohatt, Chapter Seven). This subset of patients will be extremely difficult to treat successfully, requiring ongoing clinical monitoring and trial-and-test methods to determine optimal treatment regimens. For example, patients are often in long-term settings because they respond poorly to medication. In these settings, clinical data, formatted into a multiple-baseline output, can play an important role in determining optimal pharmacological treatment regimens. By tracking multiple-outcome indicators synchronized over time, clinicians will be better able to identify subtle patterns of medication response not evident to the "naked eye," often suggesting unusual treatment combinations. The job of organizing and formatting multiple-baseline output will be made much easier by a computerized CDSS.

Second, in long-term settings, in which progress is often slow and incremental, sophisticated, continual, milieu-based clinical assessment is often necessary. These assessments can help detect changes not readily apparent by conventional means. For example, behavioral-observational measures generated by ward staff can be powerful enhancements to traditional interview and exam-based assessments (for example, diagnostic interview). When these milieu-based measures are collected on a regular basis, they can provide a rich insight into the daily functioning of patients that may be otherwise inaccessible to professional staff. However, these measures are often labor-intensive, making them prohibitive for routine use unless an efficient way of managing the data is developed. A CDSS can help make this task more manageable.

Third, in short-term settings, a CDSS can be used to help predict short-term prognosis, project trajectories of recovery, and predict posthospital needs. For example, patients with more impaired performance on a card sorting task shortly after hospitalization tend to stay in the acute-care ward longer and are more likely to be discharged to a residential or long-term unit as opposed to supported or independent community living (Spaulding and others, 1999). These results suggest that clinical data can have significant predictive utility, enabling the treatment team to better anticipate the rehabilitation needs of the patient.

Finally, a CDSS can be used to show the therapeutic benefits of rehabilitative versus custodial services, which is an important consideration with respect to the cost-effectiveness of services. Increasingly, providers of mental health services not only have to demonstrate positive outcomes but also must do so at a reasonable cost. To achieve optimum cost-effectiveness, the service system must help recipients move through a "ladder" of service settings, each having varying degrees of intensity and consequently varying costs (Figure 8.1). Recipients must be provided rehabilitation services until such services can no longer be expected to improve their personal and social functioning to a degree that would allow them to live in a less intensive setting. At that point, less costly "maintenance and support" services could be provided. The decision as to when to initiate and discontinue treatment is crucial to the efficiency of the system. Accurate decision making requires state-of-the-art clinical assessment and information management technology.

Considerations in the Development of a Clinical Decision Support System

The design considerations of a CDSS can be grouped into three categories—*system-related considerations*, *staff-related considerations*, and *administrative considerations*.

Figure 8.1. Assessment, Decision Making, and Cost-Effectiveness Ladder

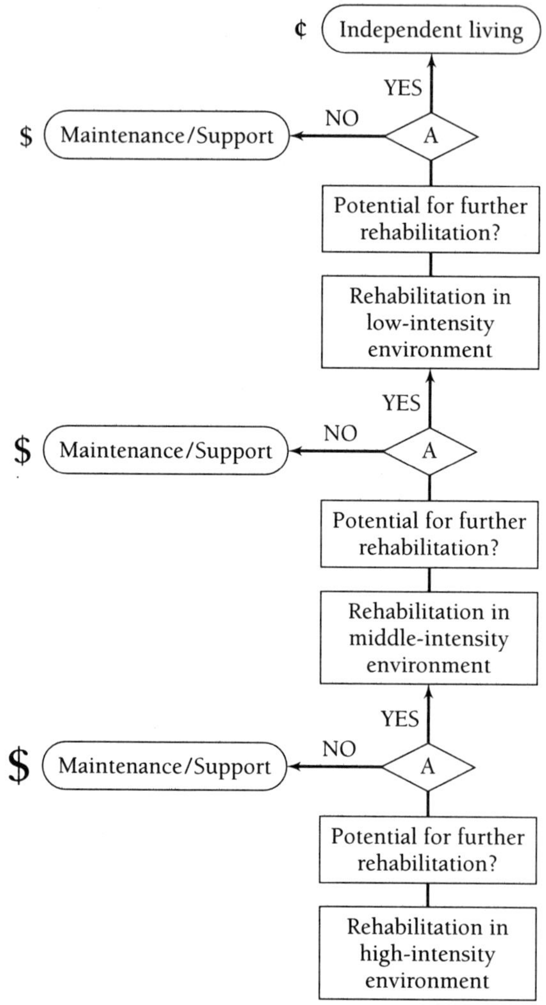

A = assessment: Optimum cost-effectiveness requires accurate assessment of rehabilitation progress and prospects for further progress.

System-Related Considerations. This category refers to the capabilities of the system with respect to data management and clinical decision making. To maximize the accessibility of the data system, a CDSS needs network computerization combined with *relational database* technology. (A relational database is one that uses dissimilar data files, organized and accessed according to relationships between its tables, records, and fields. This provides the flexibility and versatility required to manage multiple clinical measures within a single patient's master record.) Linking several computers together into a network makes it possible to keep all of the data on a single computer, the *file server*, which individuals located throughout the hospital access as needed. The benefits of a relational database are that it is capable of processing data from virtually any psychiatric measure or psychological test and returning it to clinicians in a highly interpretable format. The choice of platform (for example, Apple Macintosh versus Microsoft Windows based) is not necessarily an issue, as both platforms can be networked and most of the common relational databases (for example, FileMaker Pro, Microsoft Access) have cross-platform capabilities.

Next is the issue of measures to include in the system. The measures in the data system should be ones that lend themselves to routine repeated use in treatment planning. They should assess specific functional characteristics of patients and do so in objective and quantifiable terms. JCAHO and the Health Care Financing Administration (HCFA) mandate that goals be written in operationalized and measurable terms. Also, well-defined, quantitative measures are necessary because, during the initial design of the database, the programmer needs to specify what variables are being collected, the format of the data (for example, text versus numeric versus date), and the types of computations that will need to be performed on the data (such as computing subscale scores or summary reports). Quantitative measures also permit graphic displays of data, enhancing the interpretability of the output.

The system should include data from several different sources in the treatment setting, so that the measures assess a variety of domains of functioning. For example, the system should include observational data of behavior on the unit, ratings of attendance and participation in groups and classes, measures of cognitive functioning and symptomatology, and demographic and medication information. This is especially important when severely disabled patients are served because such patients' impairments are notoriously independent across different domains. Progress in one domain does not necessarily indicate comparable progress in another.

It is important to note that the clinical measures of most interest to system administrators are not necessarily the best for clinical assessment and decision making. Diagnostic categories, summative indicators of outcome and disposition, are good for characterizing activity across a service system, but they usually contribute little at the level of clinical decision making, especially in a state hospital population. Administrators are not always sensitive to this. In the administrative process of setting up a clinical data management system, clinicians must be prepared to insist on inclusion of appropriate clinical measures.

The system must accommodate the data management needs of short- and long-term care settings, as state hospitals usually have both. Short-term care units generally need repeated assessment of specific variables over short time frames (days or even hours), whereas long-term care units need more comprehensive assessment of patient functioning over longer time frames. Both of these needs can be accommodated in a single system by allowing clinicians to specify the time frame to analyze and the span of time over which to compile or average specific data points.

The system must have the structural flexibility to allow for the addition of new components as assessment and treatment technology evolves. This necessitates the use of a relational database programming language. In relational databases, individual variables are related through a central index that identifies the patient and the type of data stored at other locations. This permits a modular organization, and as a consequence, new variables can be added without restructuring the entire system.

Because individuals of different levels of computer familiarity and comfort will be using the system, it will be important to design the system so that it is relatively easy to use. This will keep staff training to a minimum and make it more likely that staff will use the system. However, the clinical utility of the system should not be sacrificed at the cost of ease of use. If the system is relatively easy to use but does not generate clinically useful data, or if the system generates meaningful data but is too difficult or cumbersome to use, it will not adequately support clinical decision making. In addition to being user-friendly to operate, the system must generate reports that are user-friendly in interpretation. If the output can be understood by all members of the treatment team, this will enhance its use in day-to-day clinical decision making. Similarly, the output must be effective in communication with utilization reviewers and with managed care and related administrative entities. Graphic output is a key to data interpretability. Graphs can permit efficient communication of data even to an audience whose knowledge of the specific measures is quite limited. During the initial design of the database, careful consideration must be given to formatting the output for clinicians and nonclinicians alike.

In intensive treatment and rehabilitation settings, the treatment team must often make decisions at a moment's notice, in response to rapidly changing clinical exigencies. The data system must allow for rapid processing of raw data into formatted output. In addition, quick turnaround of data enhances the treatment team's ability to develop and test specific hypotheses about patients' behavior and treatment tactics. This is a key component in the *individualization* of treatment and rehabilitation.

The system must be capable of tracking multiple interventions and outcome indicators as they change in relation to one another over time. In clinical practice, this is best accomplished by graphing several measures on a single page, in a synchronized time frame. This permits routine use of multiple-baseline data tracking, one of the most reliable and powerful ways of detecting and validating specific treatment effects.

Finally, the system should be capable of taking advantage of current networking and Internet capabilities. The importance of this design consideration is expected to increase exponentially over the next few years, as advanced communication technology becomes more accessible. Of particular interest to state hospitals and their surrounding service system is the availability of Private Virtual Networks (PVNs). PVNs make it possible to exchange virtually limitless amounts of information in time frames suitable for clinical decision making, and with security sufficient for exchange of confidential clinical data. This means that a central file server could interact with any authorized clinician working at any computer having Internet access. Entire mental health systems could easily be unified with a common CDSS and database.

Taken together, these design prerequisites make it difficult or impossible to adapt predesigned off-the-shelf database programs for use as a comprehensive clinical data management system. Administrators are often accustomed to solving management problems by making the right purchase and subsequently relying on whatever programming experience they can find among hospital staff. Retaining a professional programmer to custom-design a clinical data management system may appear to be a prohibitive expense. Nevertheless, the complexity of a relational database operating on a network in a time frame suitable for clinical decision making requires professional-level computer skills. Considering the centrality of comprehensive clinical data management to the operation and even survival of state hospitals, this must be seen as part of the necessary "cost of doing business."

Staff-Related Considerations. One of the first issues to address is training staff in how to complete the measures. Supervisors must be fully involved in this process, making sure that staff are properly trained in how to use the measures and how to ensure the ongoing, accurate implementation of the data collection. Periodic reliability checks further ensure the integrity of the data.

Staff should also be provided with some background information about measures and why they are included in the data system. One of the main resistances to data collection by staff is that they do not understand its use in clinical decision making.

Next, staff must be trained in how to use the system. The number of individuals working with the system should be kept to a minimum, and individuals should be assigned specific tasks. For example, the medical records clerk would be responsible for entering patient demographic and diagnostic information; the psychiatrist, pharmacist, or medication nurse would be responsible for entering medication data; and the psychologist would be responsible for entering psychological test data. In this way, training requirements are kept to a minimum, because individuals would only require training on specific tasks. In addition, because an individual would only be responsible for his or her own sections of the system, data entry errors or other mistakes due to unfamiliarity with some aspect of the system would be kept to a minimum. One safeguard to ensure that only authorized users are working with the system is to use password protection. Password protection can be used not only to limit who uses the data system but also to specify what components of the system different users will be able to access.

Finally, staff must not only be trained in data collection and the use of the data system but also in the use of longitudinal data in assessment and progress evaluation. Each patient's treatment regimen must be treated as a *single-subject* experiment. Staff usually need some training in the basics of single-subject methodology. This includes how to interpret intervention effects by evaluating such factors as the rapidity and magnitude of the change following the intervention, which measures change, and the variability of the targeted behavior both before and after the intervention. The data can also be analyzed for the overall importance or clinical significance of the treatment effect—what has been referred to as the "therapeutic criterion" (Kazdin, 1978).

It is important to note that despite the benefits of networking and database technology in clinical data management, computers in the mental health field continue to be underutilized. In one survey, only 72 percent of psychologists reported using computers in their practice (Rosen and Weil, 1996), with word processing being reported as the primary use for computers (Farrell, 1989; Rosen and Weil, 1996). Because there tends to be a scarcity of resources at state hospitals, computers may not be readily accessible to clinicians. Another factor that may contribute to the underutilization of computers in mental health settings deals with clinicians' attitudes toward technology. For example, in one survey, 20 percent of psychologists rated themselves as moderately to highly technophobic, and another 34 percent rated themselves as mildly technophobic (Rosen and Weil, 1996). Further, the psychologists tended to be skeptical of new technology, with over half of those surveyed saying that they would rather wait until new technology was "proven" before trying it. Another 28 percent stated that they would wait until they *must* use it.

If high-tech data management is to assume a more prominent role in state hospitals in the twenty-first century, computers will need to be utilized for more than clerical and administrative purposes, and attitudes toward technology will need to change. Clinicians must be more willing to use computers in their work, and computerization will need to be more closely integrated with the day-to-day clinical operations on the unit. Doing so will require careful attention to physical barriers (for example, access to computers) as well as attitudinal barriers (see Ager, 1991; and Farrell, 1989 for additional discussion on barriers to the implementation of computer technology).

Administrative Considerations. The administration must provide both the infrastructure and the fiscal resources necessary for the initial and ongoing development of the data system. A sufficient budget must be provided for the initial purchase of the hardware, including the installation of a network, and for access to specialized programming skills generally found only in the private sector. The administration must also be committed to ongoing data system development as an intrinsic part of program development.

Thus, during development of a computerized data management system, attention must be paid to the specific requirements for the system, ranging from what measures to include in the system to what types of output are needed. Careful consideration must also be given to training staff in how to collect, enter, and interpret assessment data. Finally, the administration must be firmly committed to all phases of this process, from the initial purchase of computer equipment through the ongoing development of the system.

A Prototype Clinical Decision Support System

In this section, a prototype CDSS is described. The prototype is based on systems that have evolved over more than fifteen years of operation in a state hospital–based intensive psychiatric rehabilitation program, the Community

Transition Program (CTP) at the Lincoln Regional Center (see Sullivan, Chapter Four, for a more detailed discussion of the CTP). The CTP is a forty-bed unit in a state hospital, with a twelve-bed transitional extension located in an apartment building in the community. Patients participate in an average of thirty-five hours per week of structured treatment and rehabilitation activities. The CTP treats chronic, treatment-refractory individuals with major psychiatric disorders, primarily schizophrenia. Patients admitted to the program come from the hospital's admission unit and various long-term settings. The average length of stay in the program is twenty-two months. Most discharge destinations are community-based residential programs, but they range to supported independent living.

A number of clinical databases and CDSSs have evolved over sixteen years of CTP operation. A state-of-the-art version, named *PsychiaTrax,* incorporates all the design considerations and the characteristics of the prototype discussed here. It was developed by and is commercially available from Sterling Database Designs of Lincoln, Nebraska.

In the CTP, CDSSs evolved parallel to development of a general model of individualized treatment planning and progress evaluation. The treatment-planning model evolved in turn from Problem Oriented Medical Information Systems (PROMIS). PROMIS is a set of medical record-keeping conventions whose evolution began in the 1960s and that is now codified in various hospital accreditation standards (for example, HCFA and JCAHO). The CTP treatment-planning and progress evaluation model adds an iterative, data-driven process to the structural skeleton of the PROMIS model (Figure 8.2).

When a patient is first admitted to the program, each discipline conducts an initial assessment. The treatment team then collectively formulates an initial case conceptualization, incorporating assessment results and any other information available (for example, old medical records, information from collaterals, and so forth). Next, the team generates a list of problems that will be used as targets for treatment. These problems are selected from a pool of formally defined problem titles and reflect the team's initial conceptualization of the patient, including etiological hypotheses. Each problem title is given a behavioral description of the problem's expression. This description serves to individualize each problem title, showing how the problem is manifested for that particular patient. Each problem title also includes a long-term goal, which reflects overall rehabilitation goals, as well as one or more short-term goals, which generally reflect approximations toward the long-term goal. Each problem also has one or more *key indicators,* operationalized behavioral measures specifically designated to assess the patient's progress toward the goals. Finally, one or more treatment modalities or interventions are listed for each short-term goal. The interventions are selected based on the team's case conceptualization and are designed to help the patient meet the short-term and long-term goals. All interventions include their own measures of service provision and patient response.

During monthly treatment progress reviews, the team reviews all data pertinent to each problem and assigns a progress rating to each long- and short-term goal. These numerical ratings are designed to reflect the patient's progress

Figure 8.2. Information Flow in Data-Driven Clinical Decision Making

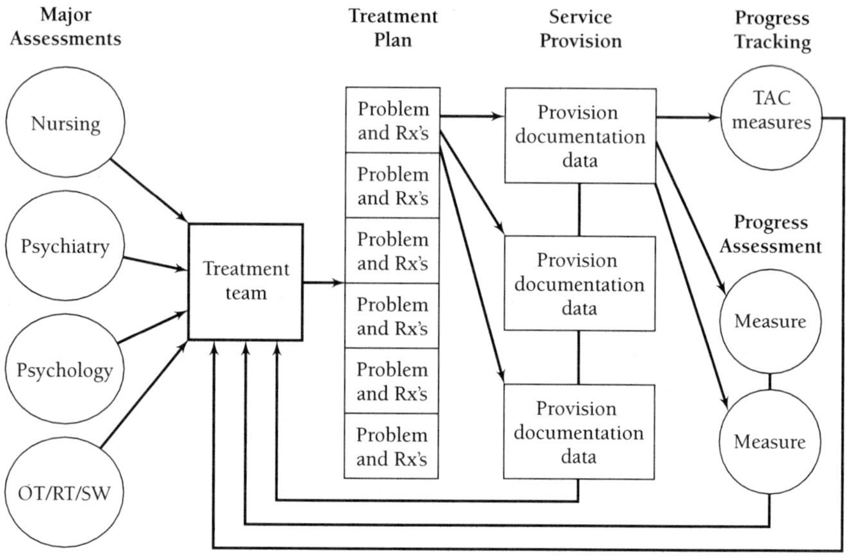

TAC = Therapy-Activity-Class

toward the goal during the review period. Whenever the team determines that a patient has not made adequate progress during the review period, the team is required to revise the formulation and treatment plan. Thus, in the CTP treatment-planning model, clinical assessment data play a key role in the initial case formulation and guide the course of treatment through formal, systematic application in progress evaluation.

In the prototype, CDSS clinicians enter data, either directly or through clerical staff. The database resides on a central file server (Figure 8.3). Each measure in the database has its own input screen along with data validation routines to reduce the possibility of data entry errors. Each measure also includes a summary report. In most cases, summary reports can display either the results of a single assessment or the results of repeated assessments summarized over a six-week or six-month time frame. Treatment plans, formulations, and progress evaluations are constructed in treatment team meetings in the course of interpreting the data, and the results are entered into the database by designated team members.

Patient Information Tracking. The Patient Information Tracking section maintains demographic and related information about the patient, such as the patient's social security number, date of admission, legal status, diagnosis, family contacts, and so forth. Output includes standard cover sheets and diagnostic summaries for the charts, census summaries, and address labels for mass mailings—for example, to family members announcing special program activities.

Figure 8.3. A Clinical Decision Support System Computer Network

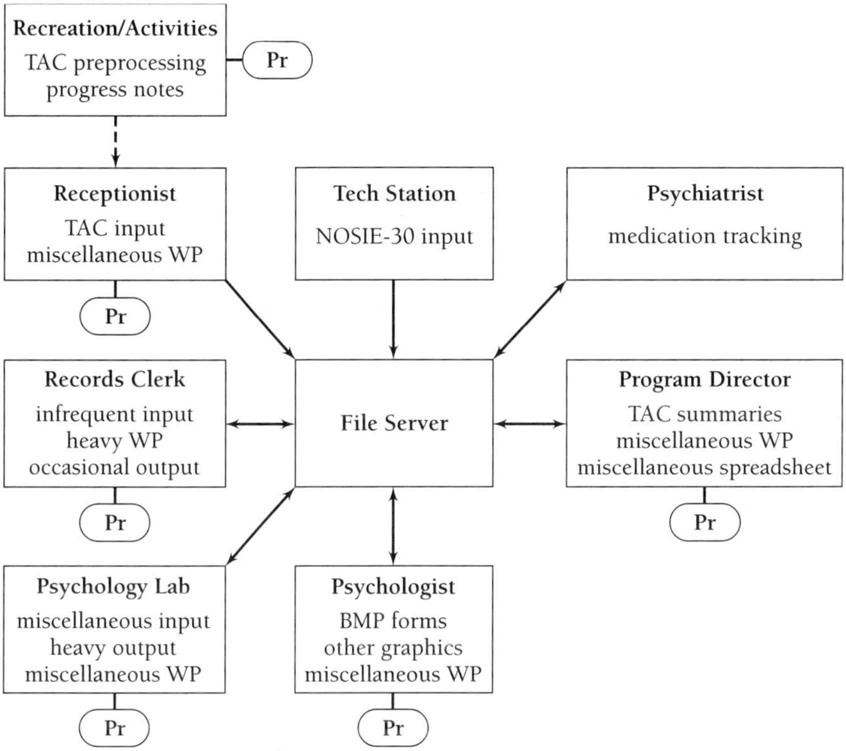

Pr = printer; WP = word processing; TAC = Therapy-Activity-Class; BMP = Behavior Management Plan

Therapy-Activity-Class Tracking. The Therapy-Activity-Class (TAC) part of the CDSS tracks provision and patient participation in all treatment and rehabilitation modalities provided in the program. TAC includes identifying data on specific modalities (name and discipline of primary clinician or group leader, scheduling information, and so forth), the patient's attendance and participation, and a behavioral-rating section to assess the quality and quantity of the patient's behavior during class.

Two types of TAC reports are generated. The first, mostly used during treatment progress evaluation, is a weekly summary for each patient that lists all of the treatment modalities the patient participated in for the week. This report is formatted for inclusion in the patient's ward chart as a type of progress note. The second report, which is used for administrative purposes, is a programwide summary that lists the total amount of treatment that each discipline and each staff member provided for the week.

Clinical Measures Tracking. This part of the CDSS can include standardized measures for assessing patients' personal and social functioning. The specific measures serve as initial assessment instruments, operational definitions of treatment goals, and independent indicators of treatment response and rehabilitation progress. Each can be formally designated as a key indicator for specific problems. The number of available measures relevant to high-intensity psychiatric rehabilitation is growing at a rapid rate, and a complete account is beyond the scope of this chapter. Measures should be chosen to span the entire range of patients' functioning. They should include interview-based measures of mental status and symptoms; observational measures of ambient social behavior; neuromotor measures for assessing medication side effects; performance-based measures of social, occupational, and independent living skills; and laboratory measures of cognitive functioning.

Medication Tracking. The Medication Tracking measure keeps track of all pertinent medication information. It lists the type, dosage, schedule, and route of administration for each medication, with dates of initiation, dosage changes, and discontinuation. Treatment teams may elect to limit this to psychiatric medications, especially when parallel tracking systems are provided by the pharmacy. The advantage of including it in the CDSS is that it permits computer-integrated analyses with all other assessment, treatment, and rehabilitation data.

Behavioral Management Plans. Otherwise known as *contingency management,* behavior management programming is often a crucial component in a comprehensive rehabilitation regimen. This is especially true for people with severe and protracted psychosis, significant neurocognitive deficits, or comorbid characterological impairment. Behavioral Management Plans (BMPs) allow for the tracking of any number of specific target behaviors, which are identified by a brief narrative description of the behavior and the environmental antecedents and consequences. As with medication tracking, this includes dates for initiation, revision, and discontinuation of specific BMPs.

Integrated Treatment Response Profile. A response profile monitors the effectiveness of the different intervention strategies across multiple domains of patient functioning. Graphically presented, it can show chronologically synchronized, treatment response data over specified time periods. This format is especially well suited to the iterative assess-trial-and-test decision process needed to successfully treat treatment-resistant patients. An example is shown in Figure 8.4. At the bottom of the example profile is a time line graph of medication history, showing medications and dosages that the patient was on during the time period. The other graphs in the profile are selected clinical measures. In *PsychiaTrax,* any single item or summary score from any of the measures can be graphed, with up to five graphs synchronized and displayed on a single page.

Conclusion

As the next millennium approaches, state hospitals will need to adopt new data management technologies in response to the demands of oversight and accreditation agencies; issues of accountability and cost-effectiveness; and the

Figure 8.4. Clinical Data Management System Treatment Response Profile

Patient: Smith, John ID: 8581
Period Ending: 12/03/98

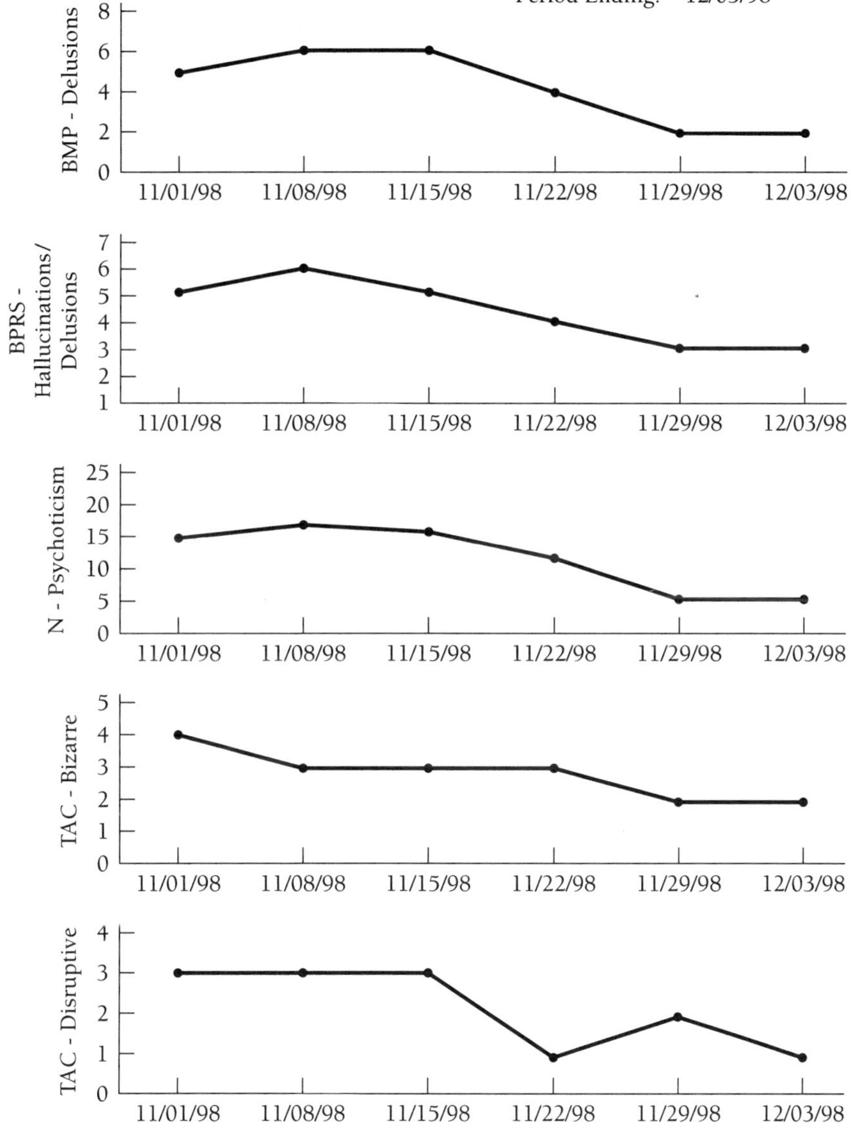

Benztropine 4 (Tab) --
Loxapine 150 (Tab) --- DISC
Risperidone 6 (Tab) --

This is a multimeasure treatment response profile.

TAC = Therapy-Activity-Class; BMP = Behavior Management Plan; N = NOSIE-30, Nurses Observational Scale for Inpatient Evaluation, 30-item version; BPRS = Brief Psychiatric Rating Scale legal, moral, and ethical imperatives to provide high quality. Computerized treatment-planning and data management models are a key to meeting these demands.

Note

1. The authors are indebted to Richard H. Hunter for this useful terminological characterization.

References

Ager, A. "The Role of Microcomputers in Clinical Psychology." In A. Ager (ed.), *Microcomputers in Clinical Psychology: Issues, Applications and Future Developments.* New York: Wiley, 1991.

Bigelow, D. "State Data Systems and Research Opportunities." In J. D. Bloom (ed.), *State University Collaboration: The Oregon Experience.* New Directions for Mental Health Services, no. 44. San Francisco: Jossey-Bass, 1989.

Farrell, A. "Impact of Computers on Professional Practice: A Survey of Current Practices and Attitudes." *Professional Psychology: Research and Practice,* 1989, *20* (3), 172–178.

Joint Commission on Accreditation of Healthcare Organizations. "Performance Measurement Systems: Evaluation and Selection." [http://www.jcaho.org/perfmeas/oryx/1pmseval.htm]. 1998.

Kazdin, A. "Methodological and Interpretative Problems of Single-Case Experimental Design." *Journal of Consulting and Clinical Psychology,* 1978, *46,* 629–642.

Paul, G. (ed.). *Principles and Methods to Support Cost-Effective Quality Operations: Assessment in Residential Treatment Settings, Part 1.* Champaign, Ill.: Research Press, 1986.

Rosen, L., and Weil, M. "Psychologists and Technology: A Look at the Future." *Professional Psychology: Research and Practice,* 1996, *27* (6), 635–638.

Spaulding, W., Crinean, W., and Martin, T. "Microcomputerized Clinical and Research Laboratories in Psychiatric Inpatient Settings." *Behavior Research Methods, Instruments and Computers,* 1983, *15* (2), 171–176.

Spaulding, W., Hargrove, D., Crinean, W. J., and Martin, T. "A Microcomputer-Based Laboratory for Psychopathology Research in Rural Settings." *Behavior Research Methods, Instruments and Computers,* 1981, *13* (4), 616–623.

Spaulding, W., and others. "Cognitive Functioning in Schizophrenia: Implications for Psychiatric Rehabilitation." *Schizophrenia Bulletin,* 1999, *25* (2), 275–290.

BRETT BUICAN is a graduate student in the Department of Psychology at the University of Nebraska-Lincoln.

WILLIAM D. SPAULDING is professor of psychology in the Clinical Psychology Training Program at the University of Nebraska-Lincoln and clinical psychologist in the Community Transition Program, Lincoln Regional Center.

BRUCE GORDON is president of Sterling Database Designs, Lincoln, Nebraska.

TONI HINDMAN is a psychological services assistant in the Community Transition Program, Lincoln Regional Center, Lincoln, Nebraska.

Readers are invited to evaluate the degree to which ideologies are influencing mental health planning and policy development activities in their own system.

State Hospitals in the Twenty-First Century: A Formulation

William D. Spaulding

This is a formulation of the future roles and functions of state hospitals, drawn from the various realities and considerations discussed in the preceding chapters. It is a "constructionist" exercise—a synthesis of clinical, technological, economic, and political issues into a unified and integrated view. The exercise is undertaken here to demonstrate the conceptual viability of such a view and its ability to serve as the rational basis for policy development and service planning in a comprehensive mental health system.

In today's somewhat polarized policy debates about services for people with the most severe and disabling psychiatric disorders, there is a view that opposes the one formulated here. A composite of that opposing view includes the following key tenets:

Virtually all people with severe and disabling psychiatric disorders can be "maintained" in "community settings," provided they have access to appropriate pharmacological treatment and to social support services that ensure they are adherent to their medication regimens and that directly assist them in performing the necessary behavioral functions of routine daily living.

The only limitation of an ideal medication-and-support service system is that it cannot completely eliminate the need for periodic brief hospitalizations or related short-term interventions in response to exacerbations (psychotic episodes) of the illness; therefore, capability to provide brief, intensive "inpatient" treatment for the purpose of neurophysiological stabilization is the only remaining necessary component of a complete service system.

State hospitals are by definition "not community-based"; if they have any role in future mental health systems, it is to provide auspices for short-term inpatient treatment, essentially no different from that provided in the private sector.

If there is any need for rehabilitative services—that is, ones that seek to improve patients' functioning as opposed to simply controlling their symptoms and compensating for behavioral deficits with extraordinary social support—they can be accomplished in community-based settings.

Of course, it is difficult to characterize complex policy premises with a few specific tenets, without creating a "straw person" to repudiate. Readers are invited to evaluate the degree to which the above tenets (or any others) appear to be influencing mental health planning and policy development activities in their own system.

The formulation constructed here holds that the opposing view characterized above (1) is not supported by outcome data, which continue to show that however effective medication-and-support services may be for the majority, there is a significant minority who do not achieve stable functioning and a decent quality of life; (2) fails to recognize the roles of judicial prerogatives, risk management realities, and the occasional need for social control in the mental health system; (3) ignores the positive outcome data on rehabilitation of people who, for whatever reasons, are confined in restrictive settings for extended periods of time; (4) makes specious distinctions between institutions and community settings, which do not differ in restriction or therapeutic value; and (5) risks replacing institutionalization in state hospitals with institutionalization in nonrehabilitative, community-based custodial facilities. However well-intentioned a radical adherence to the tenets of this view may be, in the end, it represents an abandonment of those who are unable to benefit from a favored service ideology. It leads to criminalization of people with treatment-resistant mental illness, cost shifting from the mental health system to the correctional system, and the bizarre spectacle of an underclass of psychotic street people.

The Formulation

The following is a discussion of the future roles and functions of state hospitals in a complete mental health service system according to the formulation.

The Role of Intensive Psychiatric Rehabilitation. A comprehensive mental health system must have the capability to provide *high-intensity psychiatric rehabilitation.* For present purposes, high-intensity psychiatric rehabilitation means the widely recognized array of modalities associated with psychiatric rehabilitation, augmented by additional modalities especially suited to recipients with extremely severe, disabling, and treatment-resistant disorders. This service is needed by a relatively small proportion of the entire (severely and persistently mentally ill, or SPMI) recipient population, a larger proportion of recipients of inpatient and institution-based services, and *all* recipients who need longer-term services in a moderate- to high-security environment. Although community-based programs (for example, ACT and related case management approaches) must be the primary approach for the SPMI recipient population, there must also be careful attention to complementary services for that minority of the SPMI recipient population who, for a variety of reasons, cannot access or benefit from community-based programs for extended periods of time (more than a week or two).

By definition, people in that minority subpopulation are found in restrictive settings, mostly state hospitals, but also in heavily supervised and even locked community-based residential facilities, or in the correctional system. Generally, they are there because of the environmental structure and security characteristics of the setting. The factors that create their "dangerousness" exceed acceptable levels even in the absence of exacerbations. Depending on local communities' acceptance of homelessness and psychotic street people, such individuals may also simply be ignored until they run afoul of the legal system. For both humanitarian and economic reasons, the *overriding mission* of services for recipients in this population must be to eliminate the risk factors and other reasons that keep them in such a restrictive setting, so they can access and benefit from less restrictive alternatives.

This moderate and inclusive view must not be mistaken for an endorsement of the traditional role of state hospitals. It does not imply that some people cannot escape institutionalization, nor that people should be institutionalized simply because they have pervasive deficits in living skills. It does include the premise that *anyone* can potentially come within the effectiveness range of the strongest versions of community-based services, although some may require a period of intensive psychiatric rehabilitation to do so. The *most important benefit* of an intensive psychiatric rehabilitation program is in helping people move into a less restrictive environment or setting.

Intensive psychiatric rehabilitation is the treatment (service) of choice for the subpopulation who, by not responding to even the most intensive community-based outpatient programs, find themselves in more restrictive settings. The scientific and clinical literature strongly support the efficacy of psychiatric rehabilitation in helping people with severe and disabling psychiatric disorders achieve more independent levels of personal and social functioning, *and* it can be effectively applied in the settings where the recipient population is found. In fact, the strongest evidence for its efficacy is in studies that show its superiority over other inpatient models in moving long-term inpatients into community settings (see Paul and Lentz, 1977; Paul and Menditto, 1992). Intensive psychiatric rehabilitation does not require a state hospital setting, although state hospitals often have architectural and organizational characteristics that make them well suited to being a setting for the service. With equivalent restriction and potentially higher cost, moderate- to high-security community-based residential facilities can also serve as settings.

The amount of intensive psychiatric rehabilitation needed in a service system is determined by many factors, including local judicial and psycholegal precedents and customs, the local history of public sector mental health services, and the quality and comprehensiveness of community-based services.

Progress in science and public administration technology has yielded a downward trend in the need for institutional services, but the "absolute minimum" remains unknown. The *only way* to determine the real need in any mental health service environment is to develop the best possible community-based services and to fine-tune the use of intensive rehabilitation to optimally complement those services. This is accomplished most concretely by program admission criteria that require all people admitted to the intensive rehabilitation program (or the institution) to have a clearly demonstrated history of failure to function in any available less restrictive setting.

State Hospitals as Physical and Organizational Resources. State hospitals are resources potentially capable of providing various kinds of services with optimal cost-effectiveness. This includes intensive psychiatric rehabilitation of various subtypes, fine-tuned to specific subpopulations (for example, those with dual diagnoses of Axis I-DD, Axis I-SA, Axis I-Axis II, and so forth); other specialized rehabilitation programs for other subpopulations (for example, severe SA without Axis I) needing a moderate- to high-security setting; and standard short-term inpatient treatment, perhaps specializing in recipients with acute exacerbations of disabling chronic disorders (in contrast to the typical private sector inpatient population). Developing community-based services for the SPMI population will have a defining impact on which subtypes of intensive rehabilitation are best provided within state hospitals. Similarly, local judicial and law enforcement practices could play a key role. Both of these factors are expected to change and evolve over extended periods of time, so the roles of the state hospital must evolve and accommodate as other changes take place.

An optimal configuration of state hospital–based programs helps reduce the length of stay of people in restrictive settings, keeps people out of settings that are more restrictive than they need, and enhances movement from institutional settings into community settings. Optimally, complementary state hospital–based and community-based programs are expected to look something like those diagrammed in Figure 9.1. The diagram shows an array of programs, inside and outside the state hospital (note that one is both), with arrows showing the most typical pathways of patient movement. The programs are expected to differ with respect to size, capacity, and environmental security, reflecting local demand. A key feature of this configuration is the availability of programs with finely graduated increments of restriction and intensity. This allows patients to be accommodated in environments that exactly match their individual needs, plus it facilitates the gradual movement of the most severely incapacitated patients to progressively lower levels of restriction as their progress in rehabilitation permits.

Locus and Focus. On the one hand, psychiatric rehabilitation is by its nature an enterprise that takes place in a multiplicity of settings. A modular configuration of programs within a mental health system raises the question of how specific therapies and related activities should be deployed and coordinated across those programs. State hospitals are traditionally composed of units where patients reside, as in typical inpatient wards, and where treatment

Figure 9.1. Components of a Modern Mental Health System Inside and Outside the Traditional State Hospital

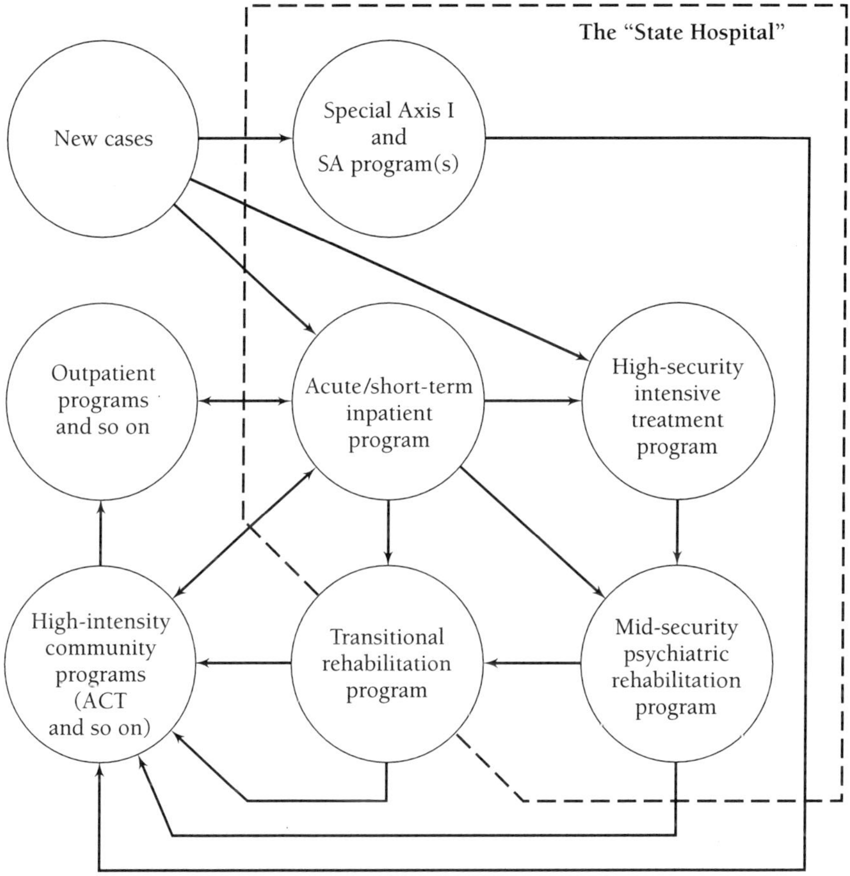

occurs. However, it is increasingly the case that state hospitals also have off-unit facilities and programs, where the bulk of rehabilitation occurs. Among other advantages, this arrangement is seen to emulate a community-based configuration, in which service recipients reside at one location and participate in rehabilitation activities at another.

On the other hand, recipients of intensive psychiatric rehabilitation services usually have significant impairments in domains of functioning most pertinent to the residential or home environment. These include basic personal care, grooming, hygiene, and housekeeping skills. Also, the recipients may be unwilling or unable to physically leave one environment to attend activities at another. Finally, risk management considerations may interact with architectural realities in such a way as to prohibit treatment in multiple locations at times.

Too little rehabilitation capability on the living unit risks the unintended consequence of allowing setbacks to interrupt rehabilitation more than is necessary. Risk factors can prevent access to specific modalities when they are only provided in lower-security settings off the living units. Similarly, having no rehabilitation on the living unit prevents optimal emulation of the environment in which living, housekeeping, and related skills are acquired and exercised—the residential environment. This also risks logistical segregation of various aspects of treatment planning and delivery, as well as diffusion of responsibility and accountability for quality services and positive outcome.

The *locus* of specific services must not obscure the *focus* of treatment and rehabilitation in *all* domains of function needing improvement. The repository of this focus must be an integrated, interdisciplinary treatment team (of which the patient is a key member). System administrators must ensure that wherever the locus, the focus is on effective rehabilitation, prescribed services are provided with high fidelity, and reliable data on recipients' treatment response and rehabilitation progress are continually returned to program administrators and the treatment teams for informed evaluation and decision making.

Rehabilitation in the Least Restrictive Environment. The recipients of intensive psychiatric rehabilitation are almost by definition involuntary patients. When community-based services for the SPMI population are state of the art, there are no voluntary patients in moderate- to high-security settings (that is, state hospitals and highly supervised community-based residential facilities). With a few exceptions, a person who consistently maintains adherence to a pharmacological and psychosocial treatment regimen can be managed and rehabilitated in a low- to moderate-security setting. Therefore, a primary goal of intensive psychiatric rehabilitation must be to engage the patient as a voluntary participant in the treatment and rehabilitation enterprise. Just as an admission criterion must be that the patient cannot function in a less restrictive setting, every patient's list of treatment goals *must include* resolution of the problems that brought about the patient's involuntary status.

The social-learning-based technologies of intensive psychiatric rehabilitation have strongly established effectiveness for resolving the problems that cause people to become involuntary patients in restrictive settings. However, like any other clinical technology, they sometimes incur short-term disadvantages that are outweighed by longer-term benefits. One of the short-term disadvantages of a social-learning approach to treatment and rehabilitation is that the patient sometimes experiences temporary increases in restriction (although such increases are small in proportion to the overriding restriction imposed by the person's status as an involuntary patient). The outweighing longer-term benefit is resolution of the problem that causes the overriding restriction, the person's status as an involuntary patient. Were the scientific evidence on the approach's efficacy not so strong, there would be more to debate. It is that strong, but it is still incumbent on the leadership at all levels of the mental health system to understand and affirm the benefits of rehabilitation and to confront simplistic arguments that neglect a realistic comparison of shorter-term restriction and longer-term benefits. Such arguments are sometimes politically appealing, as they combine superficial, misleading, and even cynical posturing about "patients' rights" with the prospect of fiscal savings through not providing services to involuntary patients.

Environmental restriction is sometimes implicitly operationalized as "length of stay," the amount of time one spends at a particular level of restriction (that is, in the hospital). This is good, as long as length of stay really does reflect meaningful differences in environmental restriction over time. The value of a shorter length of stay is in the implication that treatment is efficiently moving people to a level of less restriction, in which they can function safely and with a decent quality of life. A length of stay of one year in an intensive psychiatric rehabilitation program is "better" than one week in a short-term acute-care unit *if the former leads to a lasting improvement* in the patient's functioning and needed level of restriction and the latter only returns the patient to a chaotic revolving door, or life in the streets and jails, despite availability of the very best community-based services. Again, the scientific literature is unequivocal that intensive psychiatric rehabilitation can produce the more desirable outcome. The remaining challenge, which can be met with appropriate clinical assessment technology, is to determine which patients can be expected to experience a net improvement in adaptive functioning, autonomy, and quality of life in response to a specified length of stay in intensive psychiatric rehabilitation.

Privatized managed care raises pointed concerns in this context. Utilization review procedures adapted from management of short-term private sector psychiatric hospital use are insensitive to the potential trade-off between low-cost social support and higher-cost rehabilitation. The fiscal imperative is to put people in the lowest-cost environment as soon as possible, without regard to longer-term prospects for improved functioning. Unless managed care approaches to state hospital services are carefully reengineered, the fiscal incentive to keep people in perpetual "community-based dependency" instead of rehabilitating them may be overwhelming.

Individualized determinations about least restrictive treatment demand a more sophisticated level of clinical-psycholegal assessment than is now the norm. Even when appropriate judicial, regulatory, and oversight mechanisms are in place, it is incumbent on mental health professionals to articulate the considerations to be entered into individual judgments. This is not a function that can be relegated to administrative policy or even to oversight bodies. Assessments of individual cases must include a weighing of the shorter- and longer-term disadvantages and the potential benefits of the available alternatives for that particular case. This in turn requires a complete accounting of what treatment and dispositional alternatives are available and what factors predict the success of various alternatives for individual patients. New ideas such as therapeutic jurisprudence provide new solutions, but the limiting factor will still be the ability of mental health professionals to understand and utilize such solutions as they relate to individual cases.

Finally, a perspective that is too often conspicuous in its absence from debates about restriction is that of *risk assessment and management*. Ultimately, a patient's status is determined by somebody's assessment of that patient's risk for dangerousness, however implicit or cryptic. It is sometimes unclear where and by whom such assessments are being made in a mental health system. There need to be standards and practices ensuring that such assessments are as reliable and valid as the technology allows. This means the assessments must be done explicitly by appropriately trained and credentialed professionals exercising the best available assessment technology. The assessments must be clearly documented and available to decision-making authorities. This is another aspect of the need for a comprehensive effort to train clinical and legal professionals to use available psycholegal mechanisms more effectively.

In summary, the most defensible position on this issue is that although intensive rehabilitation in state hospitals (or comparable settings) is not *intrinsically* overly restrictive, it is vulnerable to being that in implementation. This is well recognized in the scientific, technical, and legal literature. The necessary solutions and safeguards are generally accepted, but details will always be subject to debate. Even when optimally implemented, intensive rehabilitation is vulnerable to criticisms from proponents of competing mental health system ideologies with simplistic or superficial perspectives on risk and dangerousness. A key part of the administrative task of providing humane and effective services to all people in need is to develop a working consensus about the vicissitudes of involuntary or restrictive treatment, including common understandings and efficacious mechanisms across the interface of the judicial and mental health systems.

Individualized Treatment Planning. There is a potential catch-22 in the development of effective and individualized intensive rehabilitation. In order to achieve requisite levels of therapeutic effectiveness, it is necessary to have highly operationalized procedural guidelines that staff follow in their interactions with patients (see Paul and Lentz, 1977). However, such guidelines may appear to naive or ideologically hostile observers to violate the principle of treating each patient according to his or her individual needs. Similarly, risk management considerations often make it necessary to develop policy guidelines for use in determining the appropriate level of security needed by individual patients. Policies that allow for a margin of safety in making such determinations when available information is incomplete are subject to criticisms that they are not individualized.

Development of procedure and policy guidelines must respect two key principles: guidelines are just that, and must be overridden by the treatment plan when the patient's interests and benefits warrant it; and guidelines must not be arbitrary—they must evolve in response to risk management and related factors, as they operate in a high-risk patient population. As previously discussed, risk management considerations have been underrepresented in consideration of restriction and consent.

Individualization is possible to the degree that clinicians have reliable and valid data about the individual. Inevitably, there are circumstances in which the required data are not yet available, and in such cases, conservatism on the side of safety is the appropriate approach.

How long should a patient be free of assaultive behavior before gaining a less restrictive level? How about elopement risk? These considerations are ubiquitous in the day-to-day assessment and decision making required when providing active treatment and rehabilitation to a severely disabled, treatment-resistant, high-risk population. They must be addressed whether the treatment model is psychiatric rehabilitation or anything else. The specific parameters by which safety and risk judgments are made must be highly tailored to the ambient risks in the patient population and the setting. The parameters also change over time. Determining their appropriate application in response to shifting exigencies is a continuing policies-and-procedures-development task. Some parameters are not under direct hospital control but still must inform hospital procedures (for example, how long must patients be free of assaultiveness before community agencies will accept them?). There are no universal and immutable numbers that define appropriate practice. It is incumbent on program and institution leadership to work together to evaluate the local environment and tailor clinical policy and procedures to best balance risk against restriction. Above all, these are not parameters that can be determined by vacuous application of mental health service ideologies. Individualization of treatment can be constrained by simplistic "one-size-fits-all" patients' rights policies, as well as by simplistic "one-size-fits-all" beliefs about the recipient population and their treatment and rehabilitation needs.

Conclusion

The role of state hospitals in the twenty-first century will be determined by the following factors:

The overall effectiveness and limitations of community-based programs, as indicated by current and future outcome research

Cost-effectiveness calculations that determine whether, when, and for whom rehabilitative services produce more desirable economic outcomes than services that provide maintenance, support, and crisis intervention without improving recipients' personal and social functioning

Public and political valuation of rehabilitative goals for people with severe, disabling, and treatment-resistant psychiatric disorders

Technological developments that further enhance the effectiveness of psychiatric rehabilitation in general and intensive psychiatric rehabilitation in particular

Calculations in local venues of the relative cost of providing rehabilitative services in public institutions versus private or public community-based settings having comparable levels of security and restriction

References

Paul, G., and Lentz, R. *Psychosocial Treatment of Chronic Mental Patients: Milieu Versus Social-Learning Programs.* Cambridge, Mass.: Harvard University Press, 1977.

Paul, G., and Menditto, A. A. "Effectiveness of Inpatient Treatment Programs for Mentally Ill Adults in Public Psychiatric Facilities." *Applied and Preventive Psychology,* 1992, *1* (1), 41–63.

WILLIAM D. SPAULDING is professor of psychology in the Clinical Psychology Training Program at the University of Nebraska-Lincoln and clinical psychologist in the Community Transition Program, Lincoln Regional Center.

NAME INDEX

SUBJECT INDEX

Back Issue/Subscription Order Form

Copy or detach and send to:
Jossey-Bass Inc., Publishers, 350 Sansome Street, San Francisco CA 94104-1342

Call or fax toll free!
Phone 888-378-2537 6AM–5PM PST; Fax 800-605-2665

Back issues: Please send me the following issues at $25 each.
(Important: please include series initials and issue number, such as MHS81.)

1.MHS ______________________________

____

____

$ __________ Total for single issues

$ __________ Shipping charges (for single issues ***only;*** subscriptions are exempt from shipping charges): Up to $30, add $5.50 • $30.01–$50, add $6.50
$50.01–$75, add $7.50 • $75.01–$100, add $9 • $100.01–$150, add $10
Over $150, call for shipping charge.

Subscriptions Please ❑ start ❑ renew my subscription to *New Directions for Mental Health Services* for the year_____ at the following rate:

❑ Individual $65 ❑ Institutional $110

NOTE: Subscriptions are quarterly, and are for the calendar year only. Subscriptions begin with the spring issue of the year indicated above. For shipping outside the U.S., please add $25.

$ __________ Total single issues and subscriptions (CA, IN, NJ, NY, and DC residents, add sales tax for single issues. NY and DC residents must include shipping charges when calculating sales tax. NY and Canadian residents only, add sales tax for subscriptions.)

❑ Payment enclosed (U.S. check or money order only)

❑ VISA, MC, AmEx, Discover Card #__________________ Exp. date________

Signature ________________________ Day phone ______________

❑ Bill me (U.S. institutional orders only. Purchase order required.)

Purchase order #______________________________

Name ______________________________

Address ______________________________

____

____

Phone______________________ E-mail ______________________

For more information about Jossey-Bass Publishers, visit our Web site at:
www.josseybass.com **PRIORITY CODE = ND1**

Other Titles Available in the New Directions for Mental Health Services Series
H. Richard Lamb, Editor-in-Chief

MHS83 Speculative Innovations for Helping People with Serious Mental Illness, *Mona Wasow*

MHS82 New Developments in Emergency Psychiatry, *Glenn W. Currier*

MHS81 Advancing Mental Health and Primary Care Collaboration in the Public Sector, *Rupert R. Goetz, David A. Pollack, David L. Cutler*

MHS80 Spirituality and Religion in Recovery from Mental Illness, *Roger D. Fallot*

MHS79 Building Teams and Programs for Effective Psychiatric Rehabilitation, *Patrick W. Corrigan, Daniel W. Giffort*

MHS78 Managed Behavioral Healthcare, *David Mechanic*

MHS77 Families Coping with Mental Illness, *Harriet P. Lefley*

MHS76 Developments in Geriatric Psychiatry, *Lon S. Schneider*

MHS75 Can Mandatory Treatment Be Therapeutic?, *Mark R. Munetz*

MHS74 The Successful Diffusion of Innovative Program Approaches, *Ellen Jane Hollingsworth*

MHS73 Improving Psychiatric Treatment in an Era of Managed Care, *David Mechanic*

MHS70 Dual Diagnosis of Major Mental Illness and Substance Abuse, Volume 2: Recent Research and Clinical Implications, *Robert E. Drake, Kim T. Mueser*

MHS69 Emerging Issues in Forensic Psychiatry: From the Clinic to the Courthouse, *Elissa P. Benedek*

MHS65 Clinical Studies in Case Management, *Joel Kanter*

MHS64 Assessing and Treating Victims of Violence, *John Briere*

MHS54 Neurobiological Disorders in Children and Adolescents, *Enid Peschel, Richard Peschel, Carol W. Howe, James W. Howe*

MHS50 Dual Diagnosis of Major Mental Illness and Substance Disorder, *Kenneth Minkoff, Robert Drake*